Paranoia
New Psychoanalytic Perspectives

Paranoia
New Psychoanalytic Perspectives

edited by
John M. Oldham, M.D.
and
Stanley Bone, M.D.

International Universities Press, Inc.
Madison   Connecticut

Copyright © 1994, International Universities Press, Inc.

INTERNATIONAL UNIVERSITIES PRESS and IUP (& design) ® are registered
trademarks of International Universities Press, Inc.

Library of Congress Cataloging-in-Publication Data
Paranoia/edited by John M. Oldham and Stanley Bone.
    p. cm.
   Includes bibliographical references.
   ISBN 0-8236-3985-1
   1. Paranoia. I. Oldham, John M. II. Bone, Stanley.
   RC520.P35 1994
   616.89'7—dc20
                                     93-49081
                                     CIP

Manufactured in the United States of America

Contents

Contributors

Elizabeth L. Auchincloss, M.D. is Clinical Assistant Professor of Psychiatry, Cornell University Medical School; Faculty Member, Columbia University Center for Psychoanalytic Training and Research.

Harold P. Blum, M.D. is Clinical Professor of Psychiatry and Training Analyst, New York University College of Medicine, Department of Psychiatry; Executive Director, Sigmund Freud Archives.

Stanley Bone, M.D. is Associate Clinical Professor of Psychiatry, Columbia University College of Physicians and Surgeons; Director of Education, Washington Heights Community Service, New York State Psychiatric Institute; Associate Director for Administration, Training and Supervising Psychoanalyst, Columbia University Center for Psychoanalytic Training and Research.

Arnold M. Cooper, M.D. is Stephen P. Tobin and Dr. Arnold M. Cooper Professor in Consultation Liaison Psychiatry, the New York Hospital–Cornell Medical Center; Training and Supervising Analyst, Columbia University Center for Psychoanalytic Training and Research.

Arnold Goldberg, M.D. is Professor of Psychiatry, Rush Medical College; Training and Supervising Analyst, The Institute for Psychoanalysis, Chicago.

Otto F. Kernberg, M.D. is Associate Chairman and Medical Director, the New York Hospital–Cornell Medical Center, Westchester Division; Professor of Psychiatry, Cornell University Medical College; Training and Supervising Analyst, Columbia University Center for Psychoanalytic Training and Research.

Eric R. Marcus, M.D. is Associate Clinical Professor, Psychiatry and Social Medicine, Director of Medical Student Education in

Psychiatry, Columbia University College of Physicians and Surgeons; Faculty Member, Columbia University Center for Psychoanalytic Training and Research.

John M. Oldham, M.D. is Professor of Clinical Psychiatry, Columbia University College of Physicians and Surgeons; Director, New York State Psychiatric Institute; Attending Psychiatrist, Presbyterian Hospital; Training and Supervising Psychoanalyst, Columbia University Center for Psychoanalytic Training and Research.

Hanna M. Segal, M.B., Ch.B., F.R.C.Psych. is Practicing Psychoanalyst and Teacher, the British Psycho-Analytical Society; Vice-President, the International Psycho-Analytical Association; Fellow, the Royal College of Psychiatrists.

David Shapiro, Ph.D. is Professor of Psychology, Graduate Faculty, New School for Social Research.

Andrew E. Skodol, M.D. is Associate Professor of Clinical Psychiatry, Columbia University.

Richard W. Weiss, M.D. is Clinical Assistant Professor of Psychiatry, Cornell University Medical School; Member of the New York Psychoanalytic Society.

Introduction

John M. Oldham, M.D.
Stanley Bone, M.D.

Paranoid symptoms and paranoid character traits are common yet serious therapeutic challenges. However, the understanding and treatment of paranoid phenomena and paranoid psychodynamics have received relatively scant attention in the psychoanalytic literature, considering the extent and difficulty of the problem. Reassessment, both theoretical and clinical, is timely because there are new findings in our understanding of personality organization, motivations for behavior, and self-esteem regulation. There are new therapeutic approaches to difficult clinical problems that integrate psychodynamic and sociocultural frameworks, and our theories about paranoia as a mechanism of adaptation to changing environments need reappraisal.

Freud's hypotheses for understanding paranoia emphasized the need in men and women for defense against unconscious homosexual impulses; this is essentially an extension of his libidinal model of motivation and conflict. The role of aggression as motive and the experience of helplessness in trauma were not adequately appreciated in his formulations. We know now, for example, that many paranoid patients have histories of severe abuse as children. The anticipated humiliations and chronic sense of powerlessness can lead to serious problems with the management of aggression and with the capacity for stable and robust self-definition. Cyclical behaviors may evolve that reflect "self-fulfilling prophesies" or victimization and retribution. Paranoia, erotomania, and sadomasochism may follow as elaborations.

We know that patients with paranoid problems reflect a broad spectrum of descriptive and structural diagnoses, ranging from the overtly psychotic, through the disorganized borderline, to the neurotic patients with paranoid trends and character traits, and the transient paranoid response to severe psychophysiological stress in normal individuals. Paranoia is frequently encountered in clinical work as a pervasive aspect of many types of character pathology. Projective mechanisms and projective identification are often cited among the most common primitive defenses utilized by patients with severe personality disorders. Additionally, paranoid processes occur as forces within large groups in institutional health care and within organizational and social systems.

This volume originates from the proceedings of a symposium on paranoia sponsored jointly by the Association for Psychoanalytic Medicine and the Columbia University Center for Psychoanalytic Training and Research. The focus of the volume will be on the nature of the paranoid mechanism in psychological adaptation, with particular attention to an examination of paranoid character pathology. In today's clinical work there are important opportunities to correlate psychoanalytic theory with child development, family therapy, and other areas of study such as systems theory and organizational and group psychology. This volume will include the application of current psychoanalytic thinking to these multiple arenas of psychopathology, social and organizational functioning, and clinical work.

Part I

Theoretical and Developmental Aspects of Paranoia

1

Paranoia: Historical Considerations

Stanley Bone, M.D.
John M. Oldham, M.D.

Paranoid patients, whether suffering from psychotic illnesses or simply manifesting less severe paranoid symptoms or character traits, have always presented enormous clinical challenges. Perhaps because of significant pessimism about treatment outcomes, there has been relatively little published in the psychoanalytic literature. Paradoxically, recent authors who have dedicated considerable efforts to reassessing paranoia have found themselves echoing themes that had not been fully developed by Freud, themes that originate in Freud's letters and other publications on prelibido theory. It has proved useful to elaborate the role of trauma and childhood abuse, the role of aggressive motivations, and the role of humiliation in the development of paranoia. These elaborations proceed into understanding the roles of sadomasochism and narcissism in the development of paranoia.

Modern definitions of paranoia can be traced to Kraepelin (1921) whose primary concern was with psychotic patients. Freud's work on the psychodynamics of paranoia, although evolving from his analysis of the work of the unfortunate paranoid psychotic, Judge Schreber (1911), leads to a focus on paranoid character and paranoid traits in other character disorders. Modern diagnosis of paranoid personality, clearly based on this previous work, focuses on suspiciousness, vindictiveness, problems with reality testing, and self-esteem concerns. DSM III-R (APA, 1987, p. 339), for example, utilizes the following criteria for the diagnosis of paranoid personality:

A. A pervasive and unwarranted tendency, beginning by early adulthood and present in a variety of contexts, to interpret the actions of people as deliberately demeaning or threatening, as indicated by at least *four* of the following:

    (1) expects, without sufficient basis, to be exploited or harmed by others.

    (2) questions, without justification, the loyalty or trustworthiness of friends or associates.

    (3) reads hidden demeaning or threatening meanings into benign remarks or events, e.g., suspects that a neighbor put out trash early to annoy him.

    (4) bears grudges or is unforgiving of insults or slights.

    (5) is reluctant to confide in others because of unwarranted fear that the information will be used against him or her.

    (6) is easily slighted and quick to react with anger or to counterattack.

    (7) questions, without justification, fidelity of spouse or sexual partner.

B. Occurrence not exclusively during the course of Schizophrenia or a Delusional Disorder.

We will review the historical antecedents to this current diagnostic schema. It seems important to begin with Freud's analysis of paranoia.

FREUD'S CONTRIBUTIONS

Both Blum (1980, pp. 334–335) and Gay (1988, p. 277) point out that Freud addressed paranoia prior to the Schreber case (1911) in his letters to Jung (McGuire, 1974) and in *The Origins of Psycho-Analysis* (Bonaparte, Freud, and Kris, 1954). It was not until the Schreber case, however, that Freud published his idea that paranoia represented a defense against repressed homosexuality. Freud had conceived this notion after ruminating on the character of Wilhelm Fliess (Sulloway, 1979, pp. 234–235) yet he did see the conclusion as universal. It should be noted that the Schreber case involves the analysis of paranoid psychotic symptoms more predominantly than paranoid character traits.

In *The Origins of Psycho-Analysis*, Freud began to develop many of his ideas about paranoia. He described the defense mechanism of projection (p. 111), and he saw the paranoid as defending against unacceptable impulses through the use of projection. In addition, he noted the aggressive components of paranoia, namely, obstinacy and defiance (p. 115). Even self-esteem was noted as an issue for the paranoid who was seen as suffering from pathological mortification (p. 146) and oversensitivity (p. 152). Freud's later attempt with Schreber to place paranoia squarely within the libido theory was anticipated in this earlier work, where he referred to paranoia as a sexual psychoneurosis (p. 177). While few would agree with Freud's seduction theory, that the paranoid had necessarily experienced sexual trauma between the ages of 8 and 14 (p. 177), there is much agreement today that the patient with paranoid character has commonly been a victim of child abuse.

The anticipation of attack, and the tendency to experience humiliation for seemingly trivial reasons, were seen as manifestations of problems with self-esteem, a dynamic certainly relevant to the concept of narcissism. Freud had first mentioned narcissism in his paper on Leonardo da Vinci (1910), written just prior to the Schreber case in which the important role of narcissism in paranoia was emphasized. Chronic problems with self-esteem regulation and sensitivity to narcissistic injury were proposed as a partial explanation for the vigilance and suspicious rage of the paranoid. The grandiosity of paranoid elaborations could then be seen as compensatory for chronic feelings of inferiority.

Daniel Paul Schreber (1842–1911) was a noted German jurist who documented his tragic paranoid psychosis in his book, *Memoirs of My Mental Illness* published in 1903. He was the son of Daniel Gottlob Moritz Schreber, an orthopedist and educational reformer who was well known for his idea of making "Schrebergärten," small garden plots, available to urban residents (Gay, 1988, pp. 277–284). The elder Schreber was also known for his orthopedic devices to correct

5

poor posture in children—devices that caused much more discomfort and pain than any worthwhile therapy. He is known to have used these devices on his son (Niederland, 1968, 1984).

Shortly after being defeated in an election to the Reichstag in 1884, Daniel Paul Schreber was hospitalized with delusions about his body. He remained hospitalized until mid-1885. In 1886, he was appointed a judge and evidently performed with competence for the next seven years, rising to become a presiding judge in the highest court in Saxony. Shortly thereafter, however, he became suicidal and psychotic, and he was rehospitalized until 1902. It is this hospitalization that led to Schreber's account and to Freud's explication.

Unlike many with paranoid psychoses who are guarded about the full extent of exceedingly elaborate delusional systems, Schreber documented his in voluminous detail. This detail was to serve as data for Freud in his further elaboration of a theory of paranoia. This detail was also to serve as fodder for Freud in his struggle with Adler. At the time of the Schreber case, Freud was embroiled in a controversy with Adler which split the psychoanalytic movement. Adler, who emphasized the importance of aggression, saw sexuality as much less important than did Freud. Thus, to hypothesize that even paranoia had sexual struggles at its base, was to aim one more barb at Adler, even if it meant underemphasizing the importance of aggression. The potential erotic base for paranoia had an immense intellectual satisfaction for Freud because paranoia could then fit into a universal psychology based on libido theory. It would be some years until Freud would feel obligated to develop a dual instinct theory based on both sex and aggression.

Schreber, whose term *soul murder* has resonated through the ensuing years, described delusions of persecution about his psychiatrist, Dr. Flechsig, whom he saw as a murderer of souls. Freud demonstrated that Flechsig was the object of these delusions simply because he had been so important and loved by Schreber. Freud saw Schreber's love for another man as reacted against—"I love him" becomes "I hate him." This hatred is also projected, so that the paranoid not only hates, but becomes the object of hatred. Whether or not one agrees that homosexual impulses are central to this formulation, the paranoid person does attempt to maintain an object tie. Flechsig was not lost to Schreber, since he became a persecuting object. The paranoid would rather be hated than forgotten (W. Grossman, personal communication, 1992).

Freud's elaboration of narcissism in the Schreber case is also important in understanding paranoia, even if Freud's view seemed more sharply focused on narcissism as a stage of libidinal development than as self-esteem regulation. Clearly, however, Freud's hypothesis that Schreber had regressed to a stage of predominant libidinal investment in the self does imply that Freud saw Schreber as having a problem with self-esteem regulation. Freud was to see the narcissistic stage as a developmental milestone on the way to heterosexual love. He saw Schreber's narcissistic fixation as homosexual—one developmental path for Freud was to remain fixated on one's own genitals as a love object and then to move on to involvement with others with the same genitals.

One problem in understanding Freud's notions of homosexuality is that he seemed to label some phenomena homosexual without discovering the hypothesized unconscious homosexual fantasies. For example, Freud often saw inhibition as manifesting unconscious homosexuality rather than as manifesting conflicts over aggression and struggles with self-esteem. Kardiner was quite specific about this aspect of Freud's work in his report of his own analysis with Freud (Kardiner, 1977, pp. 60, 98–100). Passivity and the wish to be taken care of implied femininity and homosexuality for Freud. These hypotheses are perilous, and they certainly led Freud to underemphasize aggression and self-esteem in his comments on Schreber's *Memoirs*.

Friedman (1988) has clarified some of the issues involved in Freud's concepts of homosexuality. Freud's ideas would now be seen as subsuming modern notions of gender related behaviors, sexual fantasies and behaviors, and gender identity into a concept of homosexuality. Today homosexuality is defined by sexual fantasy and behavior with the added dimension of unconscious erotic fantasy. For Freud, behaviors that could today be labeled as culturally "feminine" would have been labeled as typically homosexual in males.

Blum (1980, 1981) has pointed out that Freud's report on the Wolf Man (1918) is perhaps even more important than his paper on Schreber in the development of a theory of paranoia. In the case of the Wolf Man, Freud noted the connection between beating fantasies and paranoia. This is a major conceptualization because it is the beginning of the realization of the common connection between paranoia and sadomasochism. The paranoid patient is concerned with attack and counterattack, with beating and being beaten. He or she is always ready to perceive provocation, insult, or injury.

The Wolf Man's history also hints at abuse. As previously noted, abuse is a common finding in the histories of paranoid patients. What might be seen by others as persecution is sometimes rationalized by the parent and child as appropriate disciplining or caretaking. Repeated assaultive enemas, for example, were seen in one case as a medical necessity by an abused paranoid patient who was beginning psychotherapy. As with the sadomasochistic patient, aggression can fuse with libido. Repetitive abusive early life experience can become erotized and part of his ritualized adult sexual behavior.

FURTHER PSYCHOANALYTIC CONTRIBUTIONS

At the same time Freud was publishing the Schreber case, Ferenczi was arguing for anality as an explanation for paranoia. Anal sadism and the erotic investment in anality can also be seen as implying aggression in Freud's predual instinct libido theory, although Ferenczi (1911) was clearly pointing to the primary role of homosexuality. Others who pointed to anality and anal sadism in the development of paranoia were Klein (1932) and Arlow (1949). Nunberg in a paper on overt homosexuality (1938), Knight (1940), and Baumeyer (1956) explicitly wrote that aggression has the primary role in paranoia (all of the above references were noted in Frosch [1983]). Aggression was not seen by these authors as simply defending against unconscious homosexual wishes.

Frosch (1983), after documenting that aggression was seen by many authors after Freud as primary, returned to a defense against homosexuality as the primary explanation for the development of paranoia. Frosch saw the preparanoid child as experiencing humiliation from the same sex parent and experiencing any perception of passivity as traumatic. Any experience of passivity in the paranoid adult becomes equated with sadistic anal assault. The experience of passivity becomes highly conflictual—both wished for and feared. It is this experience of passivity that becomes equated with unconscious homosexuality. While Frosch's comments are thorough and sophisticated, he seems to commit the same error as Freud in equating homosexuality to a certain degree with gender labeled or related behaviors. Conflicts about passivity, and insecurity about masculinity or femininity, are not equivalent to homosexuality.

Melanie Klein saw paranoia as a ubiquitous infantile stage of development which, when not mastered, could lead to adult pathology including the psychotic disorders. Finding that Fairbairn (1946) had termed similar clinical inferences schizoid, she adopted the term *paranoid-schizoid position* for her hypotheses of the infant's experience of the first months of life. Klein saw object relations as existing from birth, with the first object being the mother's breast.

Splitting was universal for Klein, with gratification becoming associated with a "good" breast and frustration with a "bad" breast. Projection and introjection become early mental mechanisms of the infant related to "internal and external objects and situations" (1946, p. 2). Because of aggressive wishes directed at the mother's breast, the infant develops persecutory fears. In other words, the infant fears the mother will retaliate. Klein clearly saw the young infant as capable of a high degree of cognitive capability. This fear of persecution becomes crucially important, if not resolved, in the future development of paranoia or even schizophrenia in Klein's system. For Klein, paranoia had its origins in the oral phase in the first months of life as the infant struggled with his or her own aggressive wishes.

H. Klein and Horowitz (1949) in a study of eighty hospitalized paranoid patients found only few examples to support the theory that unconscious homosexuality led to paranoia. They were most impressed by the traumatic childhoods and histories of abuse found in the majority of the patients. They also speculated that some of the homosexual conflicts they uncovered were not erotic conflicts but more accurately conflicts about dependency and power. Ovesey (1955, 1969), following Klein and Horowitz, explained some of the confusion in this area with his concept of pseudohomosexuality in male patients. Pseudohomosexual struggles appear to be about homosexuality but are more accurately about the sense of masculinity. Ultimately, these conflicts have their origin in fears and wishes about issues of power and dependency. Homosexuality serves a secondary defensive function. Ovesey clearly saw homosexual conflicts as a possible source for paranoia but thought that conflicts over power and dependency were far more prevalent causes.

Vengefulness and the wish for retaliation are not exclusively aspects of the paranoid character but they are often important attributes. Searles (1956) made an important contribution in this area. Rage and the wish for revenge are common and difficult therapeutic challenges. Searles presented a series of patients, some with schizophrenia and some with paranoid character pathology, whose central problem was vengefulness. He demonstrated that in his particular cases vengefulness served as a defense against the overwhelming affects of grief and those associated with separation anxiety. The vengeful patient would rather actively seek retaliation than passively tolerate grief.

Meissner's 1978 treatise, *The Paranoid Process*, is a thorough consideration of the topic, complete with many helpful clinical case descriptions. Meissner is also of the opinion that unconscious homosexuality is of secondary importance, although he sees homosexual conflicts as commonly associated with paranoia. He focused repeatedly on aggression and patients' management of hostility. He reviewed the role of feelings of inferiority and unworthiness which he notes are defended against by paranoid projections (p. 22). He anticipated Blum's focus on sadomasochistic themes in paranoia (p. 23). He pointed to Nydes' 1963 paper which, while dealing with delusional paranoia, hypothesizes that paranoia serves to defend against guilt. In spite of the paranoid's aggressive behavior, the identification is a masochistic identification with the persecuted victim rather than a sadistic identification with the aggressor.

Blum has made substantial contributions to the literature on paranoia. He has focused the role of beating fantasies and aggression in the development of paranoia, thereby paying particular attention to the association of sadomasochism and paranoia. In his 1980 paper, Blum found Freud prophetic in this regard and he quoted from Freud's 1919 paper:

> People who harbour phantasies of this kind develop a special sensitiveness and irritability towards anyone whom they can include in the class of fathers. They are easily offended by a person of this kind, and in that way (to their own sorrow and cost) bring about the realization of the imagined situation of being beaten by their father. I should not be surprised if it were one day possible to prove that the same phantasy

is the basis of the delusional litigiousness of paranoia [Freud, 1919, p. 195].

Blum illustrated, through a description of the treatment of a male college student whom he saw in three times a week psychoanalytically oriented psychotherapy, the important role of preoedipal factors in the development of paranoia. Blum formulated the hypothesis that a profound fear of enslavement resulted from primitive underlying fears of oral engulfment as well as a wish to be engulfed. His patient had a stormy first two years of life, which included a feeding disturbance, and was followed by a remarkable insistence on preparing his own food from the ages of 3 or 4. It seemed probable that the patient's ill and disabled mother had not been available to the patient for any consistent and reliable nurturing or for that matter appropriate limit-setting and structure. The patient's father, engaged in a chronic sado-masochistic struggle with his wife, was also not fully available to his son. Blum saw the shifting identifications with both parents in this narcissistically injurious setting as relating to his patient's bisexuality and unstable identity. He did not see conflicts about bisexuality as in any way primary to the origin of the paranoia.

While Blum demonstrated the intimate association between para-noia and sadomasochism, he sharply distinguished them. He stated (1980) that: "In the perversion there is greater fusion of aggression with libido, higher level defenses and ego organization, and the reten-tion of greater capacities for reality testing and for differentiated object relationships" (p. 348). He described the narcissism of the paranoid as being much more profound.

Blum felt that during paranoid regression the patient not only sees little hope of pleasurable experience but also little hope that the threat of attack will be diminished. Motivation becomes strictly oriented toward aggressive defense and self-preservation. The best that can be hoped for is to avoid attack, or seek revenge after a perceived attack. The paranoid operates at a more impaired level of object relatedness than the masochist. Masochism can be seen as the price paid for the maintenance of an object tie. The paranoid maintains the object tie only through aggressive acts and fantasy.

Blum suggested that the loss of the object for the paranoid is equivalent to the loss of the self, since complete selfobject differentia-tion has not taken place. Annihilation anxiety becomes a commonplace struggle for the paranoid who becomes caught in a " 'vicious cycle' of fantasied injury, retaliation, and retribution" (1980, p. 351), all the while maintaining an object tie at this disturbed level.

Not uncommonly the paranoid patient suffers from depression or hypochondriasis (or both). On one level of explanation, the depression can be understood as bearing some parallels to depression in the obsessive patient. Namely, paranoid patients, in their attempts to maintain control and avoid domination, do not allow their dependency needs to be met and pay the price of depression. Early formulations of obsessive–compulsive personality understood that regressive defenses occurred along the two possible paths of depression and paranoia. The description of paranoia in pre-Schreber Freud emphasizes obstinacy and defiance which bears a parallel to the classic description of obstinacy, parsimony, and orderliness in the obsessive. Depression, paranoia, and obsessiveness are interrelated. Hypochondriasis can be understood as relating to a narcissistically damaged representation of the body. Blum pointed to Arlow and Brenner's 1969 article for further explanation. Arlow and Brenner suggested the possibility of a reintrojection of persecutory objects. The paranoid then suffers from attack which is both internalized and externalized.

In conclusion, paranoid character pathology continues to be associated with a negative prognosis, although it seems likely that continued progress in understanding will be associated with continued progression in treatment. Recent psychoanalytic work emphasizes the role of aggressive motivations in paranoid behavior and the importance of frequent histories of abuse. The long fascination with unconscious homosexual conflict was an unfortunate emphasis on a dynamic associated with only some cases of paranoid pathology. Historically, conflicts over passivity and dependency in males were invariably seen as evidence for unconscious homosexuality, whether or not erotic homosexual fantasies were uncovered. Freud saw gender role behaviors and sexual behaviors as identical. Modern authors do not ignore unconscious homosexuality in the etiology of paranoia yet neither is it seen as a central organizing theme.

Self-esteem regulation and the fear of humiliation are central issues in paranoid pathology. The self-referential grandiosity of the paranoid is a manifestation of his or her sensitivity to humiliation. Furthermore, this enormous sensitivity to humiliation makes these patients unable to be indifferent to the implications of anything in the world around them. Sadomasochistic cycles of attack and counterattack ensue. The paranoid then maintains object ties based substantially on hatred.

REFERENCES

American Psychiatric Association (1987), *Diagnostic and Statistical Manual of Mental Disorders*, 3rd ed. rev. (DSM-III-R). Washington, DC: American Psychiatric Press.

Arlow, J. (1949), Anal sensation and feelings of persecution. *Psychoanal. Quart.*, 18:79–84.

——— Brenner, C. (1969), The psychopathology of the psychoses: A proposed revision. *Internat. J. Psycho-Anal.*, 50:5–14.

Baumeyer, F. (1956), The Schreber case. *Internat. J. Psycho-Anal.*, 37:61–74.

Blum, H. (1980), Paranoia and beating fantasy: Inquiry into the psychoanalytic theory of paranoia. *J. Amer. Psychoanal. Assn.*, 28:331–362.

——— (1981), Object inconstancy and paranoid conspiracy. *J. Amer. Psychoanal. Assn.*, 29:789–815.

Bonaparte, M., Freud, A., & Kris, E., Eds. (1954), Origins of Psycho-Analysis. *Letters to Wilhelm Fliess, 1887–1902.* New York: Basic Books.

Fairbairn, W. R. (1946), Object relations and dynamic structure. *Internat. J. Psycho-Anal.*, 27:30–37.

Ferenczi, S. (1911), Stimulation of the anal erotogenic zone as a precipitating factor in paranoia. In: *Final Contributions to the Methods and Problems of Psychoanalysis.* New York: Basic Books, pp. 295–298.

Freud, S. (1910), Leonardo da Vinci and a memory of his childhood. *Standard Edition*, 11:59–137. London: Hogarth Press, 1957.

——— (1911), Psychoanalytic notes on an autobiographical account of a case of paranoia (Dementia Paranoides). *Standard Edition*, 12:3–82. London: Hogarth, 1958.

——— (1918), From the history of an infantile neurosis. *Standard Edition*, 17:1–122. London: Hogarth Press, 1955.

——— (1919), A child is being beaten. *Standard Edition,* 17:177–204. London: Hogarth Press, 1957.

Friedman, R. C. (1988), *Male Homosexuality: A Contemporary Psychoanalytic Perspective.* New Haven & London: Yale University Press.

Frosch, J. (1983), The role of unconscious homosexuality in the paranoid constellation. In: *The Psychotic Process.* New York: International Universities Press.

Gay, P. (1988), *Freud: A Life for Our Time.* New York: W. W. Norton.

Kardiner, A. (1977), *My Analysis with Freud Reminiscences.* New York: W. W. Norton.

Klein, H. R., & Horowitz, W. A. (1949), Psychosexual factors in the paranoid phenomena. *Amer. J. Psychiatry,* 105:697–701.

Klein, M. (1932), *The Psychoanalysis of Children.* London: Hogarth Press, 1959.

——— (1946), Notes on some schizoid mechanisms. In: *Envy and Gratitude and Other Works 1946–1963.* New York: Free Press, 1975.

Knight, R. (1940), The relationship of latent homosexuality to the mechanism of the paranoid delusion. *Bull. Menninger Clin.,* 4:149–159.

Kraepelin, E. (1921), *Manic-depressive Insanity and Paranoia.* New York: Arno Press, 1976.

McGuire, W., Ed. (1974), *The Freud/Jung Letters,* tr. R. Mannheim & R. F. C. Hull. Princeton, NJ: Princeton University Press.

Meissner, W. W. (1978), *The Paranoid Process.* New York: Jason Aronson.

Niederland, W. (1968), Schreber and Flechsig. *J. Amer. Psychoanal. Assn.,* 16:740–748.

——— (1984), *The Schreber Case.* Hillsdale, NJ: Analytic Press.

Nunberg, H. (1938), Homosexuality, magic and aggression. *Internat. J. Psycho-Anal.,* 19:1–16.

Nydes, J. (1963), The paranoid-masochistic character. *Psychoanal. Rev.,* 50:215–251.

Ovesey, L. (1955), Pseudohomosexuality, the paranoid mechanism and paranoia: An adaptational revision of a classical Freudian theory. *Psychiatry,* 19:341–351.

——— (1969), *Homosexuality and Pseudohomosexuality*. New York: Science House.

Schreber, D. P. (1903), *Memoirs of My Mental Illness*, tr. & ed. I. Macalpine & R. A. Hunter. London: William Dawson, 1955.

Searles, H. (1956), The psychodynamics of vengefulness. *Psychiatry*, 19:31–39.

Sulloway, F. J. (1979), *Freud, Biologist of the Mind*. New York: Basic Books.

2

Paranoid Anxiety and Paranoia

Hanna M. Segal, M.B., Ch.B., F.R.C.Psych.

Paranoid anxiety, like the poor, is always with us. I certainly have never had a patient who has not in some degree had paranoid anxieties. We are all apt to defend against guilt, loss, or even uncertainty, by looking for somebody to blame. Some potential for paranoia is necessary as a basis for discrimination. Like Freud's statement about the infant's original relation to objects: "This I shall take in; this I shall spit out," we must "taste" experience, keeping in mind the potential that it might be bad as well as the potential that it might be good. Underlying the "potential for bad" are not only our past reality experiences but also our repressed paranoid fantasies, which have to be tested by experience. Indeed, if we meet someone apparently free of paranoid anxieties or suspicions we suspect that he suffers from "antiparanoia," and is using idealization and denial to keep his mind free, possibly from paranoid anxieties too real and frightening to bear.

Of course some individuals are more prone to paranoid suspicions or anxieties than others, and it may be built into the character, and some degree of paranoid distortion invariably accompanies neurotic conditions, without amounting to what we clinically call a paranoia.

Without being unduly theoretical, this proclivity to paranoid fears has unconscious roots in infantile development. My developmental

17

view is that in the earliest phases of development, called by Klein the paranoid-schizoid position, the infant deals with the chaotic impact of external and internal stimuli by trying to order his world by splitting the object and the self into an ideal and a bad one. A crucial role in this splitting is played by projective identification, in which the infant also gets rid of whatever is a painful or bad experience by trying to project it outside into the object, thereby increasing the badness of the object. And similarly, parts of the self experienced as good and constructive may be projected into a good object, making it more ideal but stripping the ego of its potential. But in normal development, such projections are gradually withdrawn and the infant is better able to tolerate the knowledge of real objects and their good and bad character-istics, and his own ambivalence, which also leads to guilt and dread of loss. He gradually comes out of a more hallucinatory or distorted world into a world of reality, including the reality of his own desires and conflicts—psychic reality.

Defenses against this very painful situation, such as manic de-fenses, always include some regression to the prior position, some resplitting, though the splitting may take slightly different forms from that between the good and the bad; for example, it may be between the triumphant and the destroyed.

This propensity accounts for our tendency to relapse into states of mind accompanied by paranoid anxieties and suspicions due to a regression to the paranoid-schizoid position, as I have described, but which are still subject to reality testing. The projective identification is at the root of it, but it is more flexible and more easily withdrawn. It allows the existence of doubt, in contrast to the absolute conviction characteristic of the psychotic delusion. Somewhere at the core there is usually a more psychotic situation which can at times be mobilized and, partly at least, modified in analysis, but it exists in a deeply repressed state in an otherwise nonpsychotic though disturbed person-ality.

Mr. X was a rather paranoid personality. He was suspicious and quarrelsome with men, particularly those in authority, got on badly with his wife, toward whom he was rather paranoid. Though devoted to his children, and on the whole a very good father, he felt readily persecuted by their demands. At some time in his analysis he reported a recurring dream, which he had had ever since he could remember:

In the dream he is in a half-lying position, tied to a chair, surrounded by elongated animals with huge toothy jaws.

He identified the animals as resembling crocodile jaws. This dream kept recurring in the analysis in various contexts. At times it was associated with fears of castration; at other times with fear of unborn babies inside his mother, containing a projection of himself. The last version of the dream, after which it stopped repeating, we could understand as the truly psychotic relation to a devouring part-object, actually located in the gastric symptoms from which he suffered.

One day I was struck by his own half-lying position as if being tied to a chair, and it occurred to me to ask him if he had ever been swaddled. It turned out that he had been swaddled till the age of 4 months and had suffered from a great deal of colic. He was a screaming baby. It seemed to me that swaddled and deprived of movement and of any possibility of motor discharge, he was particularly prone to violent projections, vested maybe in his scream, making him live in a world in which he was surrounded by projections of his bodily experience of immobility, maybe some visual experience of the bound-up lower part of his body (the elongated shape), and his mouth—hungry, screaming, wide-open, biting—which must have felt enormous to him. After that session the dream disappeared, and insofar as I remember, it was then that the gastric symptoms began to subside.

Contrast that with an adolescent hebephrenic patient I had in treatment. One day, following a phase of considerable improvement, she came into the room dancing, twirling, muttering incomprehensibly, and making gestures of throwing something round the room. The gayer she was the more depressed I found myself feeling. Noting that in her better phases she was a great reader of Shakespeare, it struck me how much she resembled Ophelia strewing flowers. When I suggested that, she immediately calmed down, after saying sadly "But Ophelia was mad, wasn't she?" Getting in touch with thoughts about the death of her father was felt by her as a terrible persecuting dead body inside her. In fragmenting and dispersing the flowers, my patient was minutely fragmenting a dead object and her perceiving self, and projecting confusion and depression into me.

Both patients reacted to the approach of depressive feelings by a reawakening of paranoia. But both the symptomatology of the patient and the nature of the transference were very different. The way of understanding the first patient was through his dream and associations. Whilst with the hebephrenic it was through her actions and my counter-transference. Both patients reacted to situations of stress, and particularly guilt, by a regression to a paranoid-schizoid position. I think the difference was basically in the nature of the paranoid-schizoid position that they regressed to.

Since Klein's first formulations about the paranoid-schizoid position, many of us, particularly those working with psychotics—Bion (1957), Rosenfeld (1971), Sohn (1985)—began to discriminate between various aspects of projective identification. In particular, we began to discriminate between more or less disturbed forms of projective identification. Bion distinguished between projecting whole parts of oneself into the object, more easily reintegrated; and what he called pathological projective identification, in which the infant attacks and fragments his ego with great violence, and those fragments are projected into the object, fragmenting it so that it becomes what he calls bizarre objects, fragments of objects containing fragments of ego imbued with extreme hostility. This is like the fragmentation of the self into the scattered flowers by my Ophelia patient.

A similar scatter was shown by another patient of mine, who had a hallucination of being attacked by thousands of little computers possessing his brain. The thousands of computers invading his brain we identified first as my interpretations, but those computers were also returning fragments of the results of an omnipotent fantasy he had which ran for weeks, having to do with installing computers in all the schools through which he would be able to control all the education in England. Fragments of himself were supposed to be lodged in every school of the country. Bion (1957) describes the bizarre object as a fragment of the object containing a fragment of the projected ego imbued with great hostility. That is what the patient's computers were—a bit of him inside a bit of me invading his mind with the utmost hostility.

But this fragmentation is only one possibility of a bad relation between what Bion called the relation between the container and the contained. I think clinically one can detect the move from paranoid anxiety to paranoia partly by the degree to which not only impulses and fantasies, but the judging parts of the ego, are projected into the object, robbing the subject of his mind. My patient vested his intelligence and judgment in the computers, which then came back to judge him.

20

I think it also depends on the degree of completeness of identification, that is, the degree of omnipotence. When the infant projects into the parental figure, if he retains an idea of being contained there, even if he attributes to the container some of his own characteristics, like dangerous greed, hostility, or possessiveness, if the mother's response is one of understanding the projection may be loosened and reinternalized, modified by understanding. But if the degree of identification is such that the experience of containment is totally lost and the object just becomes completely identical with the self, modification short of understanding that process is not possible. This makes it extremely important technically to interpret it at the right level, and certainly not to attempt to reverse the projection by a simple interpretation of projection.

This is shown very neatly by an interpretation made by a supervisee of mine. A patient had been on the clinic waiting list for a long time, having originally come with anxiety about being homosexual. In the meantime, unknown to my candidate, the patient had become psychotic. When, after a short preliminary interview, he came to his first session, he glared at the couch and said: "I will not lie down for you. I lay down and submitted to men often enough." His looks and his demeanour, as well as the communication, clearly conveyed that he was in a completely deluded state. The candidate responded by saying: "You are afraid that I shall not be able to distinguish between psychoanalytic treatment and buggery." This communication made the patient relax almost immediately, and the psychoanalytic process had started.

The candidate picked up immediately not only that the patient himself made a concrete identification between lying on the couch and analysis and his homosexual experience; he also understood that the confusion was projected by the patient into him; that is, not only was the homosexuality projected into him, but also the psychotic functioning itself. Later in the treatment it appeared that in the waiting period, unable to tolerate the waiting, the patient did have his first homosexual experience and became psychotic after it. He obviously equated the first session of analysis with his homosexual experience.

The experience of this patient was very concrete, in keeping with my description of concrete symbolism and Bion's description of the alpha and beta elements (1963). According to Bion, the infant's first

21

experience is largely made up of what Bion calls beta elements—inchoate, fragmentary, and concrete elements of experience. The only thing the infant can do with them is to project them outwards into the maternal breast. If the mother responds adequately to this experience of anxiety projected into her, the infant can reintroject those beta elements, converted by mother's understanding into alpha elements of thought and feeling. He can also introject the maternal container, the mental space, and the mother's alpha function, which is the ability to convert beta into alpha. Operating on beta elements is the hallmark of psychotic thinking.

I want to illustrate how this process of conversion of alpha into beta can also be reversed.

The patient who had the computer episode had been in analysis with me for twelve years. He had had two severe psychotic breakdowns, one right at the beginning of the treatment, necessitating hospitalization for several weeks, and one, later, for only a couple of days. Since that time he had a few psychotic episodes: the one about the computers some years ago, and a more recent one two years ago. All these were contained in the analysis, and he showed considerable improvement in his personality and the quality of his life in general, with great improvement in his professional life and considerable changes in his sexuality.

The last episode, which happened during his wife's pregnancy, was connected with bad and fraudulent building work on his attic, which he had undertaken in a very manic way. It led to the collapse of the roof, and the patient had a short and violent manic episode followed by deep psychotic depression. Both mania and depression were accompanied by violent paranoia and delusions about his builders, and enormous murderousness toward them.

Since then, his fear of madness was often contained in dreams about flooded houses, collapsing roofs, and attics. It is important to know that ever since he entered analysis this patient had been planning to write a book on psychoanalysis, philosophy, and language, where he would put all the great theories that he admired in their place. Even though his intellectual functioning had improved, and in fact he had written many interesting articles during his analysis, the book was still the great aim.

On Friday he had a dream. In the dream there was a dinner party and he was sitting opposite me. R was also there, sitting on a potty and looking self-important. Some time during the party a small child started screaming and I was trying to deal with him in a very competent and professional manner. In fact R had just published a book which was the object of great envy for the patient; and the patient, together with some other friends, were organizing a party for R. He had also heard in the past from friends about a dinner party at my house, at which R was a guest. Sitting on the potty was very much linked with the patient's past, in which his omnipotent attitude was often depicted in dreams as sitting on a pot like a king on a throne and producing marvelous, huge stools.

I will not go into the details of that session, but the dream was clearly a reversal of both the party for R's book and the party many years earlier which R had attended at my house. The party was for my patient and the excluded-child part of the patient (the weekend) was split and projected. His real feelings were put into the screaming child, and his omnipotent "king-on-the-pot" self into R.

The patient was quite able to follow my interpretations and much of the dream was understandable to him, and the emotions were quite vivid. At some point he shouted "It's my party, so I can do what I please with it!"—and then felt abashed as I pointed out to him that the actual party was supposed to be for R with his, the patient's, help.

I shall present the Monday session in a fair amount of detail, to show why this patient, who on Friday functioned on a very neurotic level, was, and may be still, threatened by a return of psychosis.

He was a few minutes late, which always worried him, and said he was late because he was browsing in a bookshop. (This is still connected with the book; he was planning to apply for a grant to give himself time to get on with it, but had gradually begun to think in the sessions that his research project was still very vague and grandiose, and that even if he did get the grant he would feel very fraudulent about it.) He was also delayed by a deaf man asking him for directions in the street as he left the Tube.

He then said that the weekend was quite good, but he felt worried because his dreams, which seemed to him good to begin with, became very troubling later. In the first dream there was some flooding in the house. A small pipe was leaking in the attic, but he found some simple wooden gadget with which he could hinge the pipe and then direct it to a big pipe outside. Later on in the dream he was looking at a model. He was on the way to take an examination, and looking at the model

23

he wondered whether it was really good enough to sustain his research plan.

He then had a few associations, first about the relief that the pipe stopped leaking; and to the Friday session, in which he thought that the links I made about his dream of the party brought him great relief. That must have been the wooden gadget. He then had some associations which sounded to me perfunctory and bookish about the pipes being maybe small and big penises. (He was very given to such bookish associations, and yet at the end of the session I realized that they also had a deeper significance.) The gist of our understanding of these two dreams was that after feeling unhinged he felt hinged again, and this enabled him to take a saner look, not only at the model of his book but at the model of his mind, and he was more willing to examine it more critically.

But the next dream he said was very much along the old lines. And then it became very fragmented and he woke up very worried. He was sitting beside Susan. They were joking about content. He did not know what the joke was. But when he woke up he felt very uneasy about it. Susan was married to C, one of my patient's great intellectual heroes. My patient knew her before she was married and he associated that he felt he had some power over her because of the things he knew. She told him that her first boyfriend had left her because he was put off by her screaming at the point of orgasm. He also held it against her that she was Jewish and hid the fact from his friends. The patient felt also guilty toward her because he had made a nasty anti-Semitic joke about her. When she borrowed a book from him he told friends that she got her books the Jewish way. He himself got several books recently the same way. He did not like Susan. She was very envious of her brother, but used the fact that her brother wrote a book to bugger him, the patient, with. He was also very jealous of Susan being married to such a man as C. He immediately recognized that Susan's screaming at orgasm must have something to do with the screaming child (himself in the Friday session and over the weekend). And he was again confronted with a most enviable couple: R as my dinner guest and Susan married to C. The woman screaming at orgasm is very significant because the patient used to be very promiscuous in a very cruel way, projecting the screaming into women by his sexuality.

After some talk about this dream, he returned to the weekend. His daughter, Susie, was not very well and he got up several times to look after her. He had the usual worry of being either too brutal or too seductive. He then had very fragmented and troubled dreams. His first dream was about Susie. She was horribly mutilated by someone having raped her vaginally and buggered her with some wooden peg. Then he was looking into the mirror and found some horrible growth in his ear. He associated the rape and buggery of Susie with his usual anxiety about his relation to his daughters and the looking into the mirror he connected with his habit as a child and as an adolescent of trying to see his anus in the mirror, a very complicated gymnastic procedure, and also to the fact that he often masturbated anally with a wooden brush. He had not noticed two significant features: one, that Susan and Susie have the same name; and, two, the reappearance of the wooden peg—a link to the first dream of the very helpful wooden gadget.

He was again, as on Friday, faced with the enviable couple, particularly in this case envy of me as the woman who made helpful interpretations, and he dealt with it by a violent intrusion, raping and buggering me, converting the grown-up Susan into the dependent child Susie. He also chose a woman, Susan, into whom he could project his screams by raping and buggering her, and filling her with envy. This is accomplished by the wooden gadget. I think this in a way is the crux of the dream.

The Friday session was felt by him as me making links which were emotional and mental. This brought him a great relief, and he was able to subject his own state of mind to an examination. But the same wooden gadget which played this helpful role in the first dream became his possession and completely concretized: it became a wooden gadget with which he could bugger me up. The association to penises earlier in the session was an attempt to do that: fill my mind with penises. The alpha element had been transformed back into a beta element. The mental link became the concrete object, both his possession and an element that can only be used for projection.

It may seem that I have chosen a very insignificant element of the dream to which to attach so much importance, but it seems to me very much the crux of the matter. The patient could be helped to function in a less concrete way, but there was still a core of beta functioning, and, under the stimulus of deprivation and increase of jealousy and envy, he reverted to it and transformed the alpha elements back into beta.

You could say that, like the psychosomatic patient I mentioned, this patient still communicated with me through dreams and associations. Nevertheless, he himself was very aware that his dreams were still "blueprints for acting out." They defined how he was going to function during the day. The acting out in this session was minimal: being delayed by the books and the deaf man. But he still spent a large part of his time living in an imaginary world, and recently he had spoken of living in a world of duplicates, the duplicates being a combined him and me, a sort of hybrid figure which he projected everywhere.

But to return to the paranoia, the dream of Susie revealed that in his fantasy he turned me into this buggered-up child; but the dream about his ear was a paranoid dream. The growth in his ear was the same as the computers. It was my words that became a cancer in his ear. But he did not let those words in. He formed in his ear a sort of beta-element screen that prevented my words from penetrating any deeper. It was truly a deaf man that had made him late for the session in which he would have to listen to my words.

REFERENCES

Bion, W. (1957), Differentiation of the psychotic from non-psychotic personalities. *Internat. J. Psycho-Anal.*, 38:266–275.
———— (1963), *Elements of Psycho-Analysis*. Northvale, NJ: Jason Aronson, 1983.
Rosenfeld, H. (1971), Contribution to psychopathology on psychotic states; the importance of projective identification in the ego structure and object relations. In: *Melanie Klein Today*, Vol. 1, ed. E. Spilling. London: Routledge, 1988.
Sohn, L. (1985), Narcissistic organization, projective identification and the formation of the identificate. *Internat. J. Psycho-Anal.*, 66:201–213.

3

Paranoid Character and the Intolerance of Indifference

Elizabeth L. Auchincloss, M.D.
Richard W. Weiss, M.D.

No state of mind more poignantly illustrates the nature of basic human needs than does the state of paranoia. In our private paranoias, we can observe how as individuals we hunger for knowledge, demand control, struggle with passions, and above all, insist on feeling connected with other members of the human mass.

In his remarkable book, *The Great War and Modern Memory*, Paul Fussell (1975) tells us that British soldiers in the trenches of World War I believed that farmers "living just behind the lines [of battle] signaled the distant German artillery [about the position of allied emplacements] by fantastically elaborate, shrewd and accurate means." According to Fussell, "so much ploughing was always going on behind the lines that it suggested a host of variations on signaling techniques [including] ploughing in view of the Germans with white

---

In the interests of narrative clarity, material from the clinical situation is reported in the first person singular. Except where noted by the initials (RWW), the patients described were in treatment with Dr. Auchincloss.

This chapter appeared in the *Journal of the American Psychoanalytic Association*, Volume 40, Number 4, 1992. It is reprinted here with the permission of the editor.

or black horses on different occasions" (p. 120). In this vignette, we can easily imagine the homesick young soldier, terrified for his life, and helpless to know of or control his fate, who prefers the experience of betrayal to the emotionally intolerable possibility that the simple farmer might be indifferent to his plight.

The need to feel connected with others is universal. In situations of extreme threat, as in the trenches, our need to feel connected may take concrete forms. In a more benign example of the need to feel connected, Fussell tells us that troops on both sides of the lines enjoyed imagining that the entire trench system might be interconnected, that one might walk underground from the Belgian coast to the Swiss border, or send a joke to be enjoyed uninterrupted along the same route. The sense of being physically connected with others was comforting and fortifying.

In different but equally concrete ways, we may seek to feel connected with others with our thoughts. We feel connected if we imagine that another is thinking the same thoughts as we are or if we know, or think we know, precisely what another is thinking. At the simplest level, we feel connected if another is at least thinking *about* us or, conversely, being thought about *by* us.

Fussell's vignettes about trench life remind us that anyone may become paranoid in the setting of severe disruptions to security or to connectedness with others. There are those individuals whose ongoing sense of security and connectedness is so fragile that paranoia is a chronic condition; if stable enough, that condition becomes character. There are also many individuals whose character simply has a paranoid aspect.

In individuals whose paranoid ideation is significant, the issue of connectedness is always important. Exposing the barriers to feeling emotionally connected, and exploring the fantasies which ensure feeling connected, are crucial to understanding the paranoid state of mind. The paranoid person is always at the mercy of connecting to the object world through special kinds of thoughts that nonparanoids resort to only in times of stress. Such special thoughts of connectedness are reflected in the following kinds of comments typical of paranoid patients: (RWW) "I never had to worry what my father was thinking, I always knew he and I thought the same exact thing"; "There are different kinds of silences in this room, right now I know that you are judging me"; "If I don't change the wording of what you say, your ideas will be in my head and you'll be able to control me''; ''All I can think of is what I know you want me to say.''

The paranoid relies on concrete experiences such as thinking the same thoughts as another; on fantasies of knowing what another is thinking; or on the experience of being thought about by or thinking about the object. To experience emotional connectedness to an object reflects a complex achievement in internalized object relations which is not available to the paranoid. Paranoids lack the ability to maintain a loving attachment to the internal representation of an object in the face of intense frustration or rage toward that object—the ability known as *object constancy* (Panel, 1968). Lacking object constancy, the paranoid's ability to love is unstable; he attempts, therefore, to avoid *feeling* attached to objects, imagining instead that he can maintain and control connections with objects by thinking about them in magical, concrete ways. Many paranoid persons are, in fact, so dependent upon concrete fantasies of connectedness to objects that any experience, however fleeting, in which he is not thinking about the object or being thought about by the object in some magical connecting way is experienced as identical with total emotional indifference. In paranoid persons, if self and object cease to think about each other, the thought which connects them is severed. Self and object are preserved, but the meaningful connection between them is destroyed. Self and object ''float through space,'' as one patient dreamt, ''like silent space ships, gliding past each other in a calm, indifferent night.'' The paranoid so dreads this possibility of utter indifference that he insists on feeling connected to objects in concrete ways that severely limit his freedom, and paradoxically, makes attempts to connect through feeling even more dangerous. Because of this last paradox, which will be discussed further, it is vital to interpret the paranoid's rigid reliance on magical connectedness to objects before the problems of love and hate can be managed.

PARANOID CHARACTER AND THE PROBLEM OF OBJECT CONSTANCY

In 1911, Freud explicated his theory of paranoia in his discussion of the Schreber case. Freud understood Schreber's persecutory delusions concerning God and his physician, Flechsig, as a defense against the awareness of homosexual wishes. In his argument, Freud cited Schreber's delusional conviction that he was to be transformed into a woman to be sexually abused and impregnated by God. Freud also observed that the relationship between Schreber and God seemed to be modeled on that of a son and an ambivalently loved father. The persecutors who figure in paranoid delusions, Freud concluded, were formerly beloved. Although Freud did not comment on this aspect, Schreber's description of his relationship to God is striking for its profound intimacy and omnipresent quality. Schreber and God were in contact by one means or another all the time.

In his 1940 paper, "The Relationship of Latent Homosexuality to the Mechanisms of Paranoid Delusion," Dr. Robert Knight (1940) focused on the paranoid's primary struggle with aggression. He understood the paranoid's intense wish to be loved, expressed in the fantasy of homosexual surrender, as the wish for reassurance that his aggression has not destroyed the object and that the object does not wish to retaliate. The homosexual wish is warded off because, "the least approach to the object in a homosexual way arouses intense anxiety that both the object and himself will be destroyed by [the] hostility" (p. 153). Still theorizing within the confines of drive psychology, Knight concluded that at the core of the paranoid's pathology were intensified anal-sadistic wishes and passive anal yearnings.

More recently, Dr. Harold Blum (1980, 1981) has enriched the theory of the paranoid dilemma. He has integrated observations regarding the separation–individuation process with ego psychology and object relations. He has accurately noted that the psychopathology of the paranoid character cannot be explained as the consequence of a struggle over libidinal or aggressive drive derivatives. Rather, paranoid pathology is embedded in organizing fantasies which condense a number of ego distortions with preoedipal and oedipal conflicts. Blum noted that at the core of paranoid pathology is the lack of object constancy. Constant contact with the object is one response to this inability to maintain object constancy with regard to an object representation. This paper is an elaboration of Blum's views, with a focus on the fantasies of connectedness to the constant object.

In 1970, in a landmark paper entitled, "A Psychoanalytic Classification of Character Pathology," Dr. Otto Kernberg (1970a) suggested that character pathology may be divided into two groups based on overall level of "defensive organization of the ego." At the lower level, splitting is the primary defense mechanism and is thought to reflect severe pathology of the internalized object relations in which *object constancy* has not been established. According to Kernberg, this lower level, or borderline personality organization, includes many character types previously classified at the descriptive level only, including narcissistic, antisocial, "impulse ridden," "as if," "inadequate," hypomanic, schizoid, and paranoid personalities.

In other work dating from the same period (1970b), Kernberg describes how character traits in the narcissistic personality reflect the fantasy of a grandiose self in which the representations of self, ideal self, and ideal object are fused. By maintaining this fantasy of a grandiose self who does not need others, the narcissist avoids the terrors of an inner world where object constancy cannot be maintained. According to Kernberg, the pathological grandiose self can be understood as a secondary structure which serves to manage the underlying primary structural problem of the lack of object constancy.

Using a similar approach, this paper will treat the fantasies of magical connectedness central to paranoid character as secondary structures which serve, as does the grandiose self of the narcissist, to protect the paranoid from the anxieties of object inconstancy. In our opinion, this extensive defensive use of concrete and magical fantasies of connectedness to objects is the *essential* characteristic of paranoid character. Clinically, these magical fantasies are reflected in paranoid ideas and feelings of reference with regard to the object world, accompanied by feelings of *conviction* about what those objects are thinking. Paranoid fantasies of connectedness represent partial "defensive refusions of self and object representations," of the type described by Jacobson (1964); because they are secondary defensive structures, they do not represent a fixation at a "paranoid position" (Klein, 1946) or a primary failure to differentiate between self and object; they do, however, make the paranoid person more vulnerable to psychosis.

We should also clarify that while we share Kernberg's views on the presence of these defensive structures, we do not feel that understanding the psychopathology along these lines commits us to a particular developmental schema or an emphasis on the early origins of severe psychopathology. Moreover, this line of understanding does not preclude an appreciation for the role other factors may play in the development of paranoid character, such as indentification with a disturbed parent. We use the term object constancy to refer only to pathology in object relations in the present and not to any developmental stage. We do not see either the experience of object inconstancy or the fantasies of connectedness constructed to deal with it as the reexperience of early childhood mental states.

It is impossible not to note that this formulation of the paranoid character is remarkably similar to Freud's formulation at the end of the Schreber case (1911). There, Freud suggests that paranoia involves a withdrawal of all libidinal cathexis from a previously loved object onto the self in a narcissistic retreat; delusional symptomatology is seen as a secondary attempt to recover the object tie. In our formulation, however, the object from whom the paranoid withdraws and to whom he then seeks to reconnect, is not an object previously loved but one whom he is *unable* to love in a stable way.

Clinically, only when self-reference and conviction about the object are experienced benignly (i.e., unaccompanied by feelings of persecution), as in the kind of quiet paranoid most likely to be in analysis and exploratory psychotherapy, is the analyst able to observe the patient's extensive use of these magical systems of connectedness in their pure form and with their original purpose of maintaining a connection when loving attachments are unstable. When these systems of connectedness fail in this purpose, which they inevitably do at some point, they become malignant, or permeated with rage, intensified through the use of splitting. At this point, persecutory paranoid ideation predominates. In persecutory ideation, these special pathways of connectedness become pathways for attack. If the pathways of connectedness become permeated with feeling, but the aggression is split off entirely, the result may be euphoria or erotomania.

For example, a patient, Ms. A, described how persecutory paranoid ideation could alternate with blissful euphoria, almost erotomania, in the same session. Both states of mind made use of the same fantasy of magical connectedness: the fantasy that the analyst was in her head. Ms. A was a 52-year-old single business executive who came to analysis because she had never had a relationship with a man. Warm, friendly, and girlish in appearance, she was popular and successful at work. She maintained many long-standing friendships with women, although she was known for having crying fits during which she felt certain her friends did not like her. She felt "totally awkward" with men, completely unable to "be myself." In analysis she quickly revealed that her predominant train of thought concerned what others were thinking about her, with marked ideas of reference. These thoughts had the quality of conviction, not fantasy. She had similar preoccupying convictions about the analyst in the transference.

In one session Ms. A complained about being "forced" to free associate. "If I tell you everything I'm thinking, you will be inside my head," she said, through angry tears. "I'll be invaded and controlled. I hate it. I don't think I can do it." Although Ms. A had said this before, as have many patients, for some reason, on this occasion, it dawned on me how concretely she experienced my being inside her head. I pointed out to Ms. A that she did not seem to distinguish between my being extensively informed about her experience, from my being literally inside her head. This was true, she agreed, and she went on to insist angrily that she would not tell me everything. Then, in an apparent change of heart, she reminded both of us that she did not always feel angry with me. "On weekends, when I cannot see you, I think of you constantly," she said. She had told me this before but had not been able to tell me much about the content of this "thinking about" me. "At those times, I am not angry, but I feel blissful and happy. I feel that you really love me." I pointed out to Ms. A that by saying she thought of me constantly, she might again be saying that she felt I was "in her head" at those times too. "Absolutely," she agreed, "only the feeling is the opposite. It is wonderful." I pointed out to Ms. A that as long as she felt it was possible for me to be inside her head, which suggested the possibility that some of our separateness would be lost, I could certainly understand how she was subject to such extremes in mood, depending on how she felt about me while we were so intimately connected. I suggested it might be important to understand more about the idea that I *could* be in her head. Ms. A was curious but she was also puzzled. "If people don't get inside each other's heads," she asked, "how do they relate to one another?" I realized that for her, this question was a serious one.

If paranoids invent systems of magical connectedness to avoid having to deal with love and hate, it is clear that they almost always fail. As Ms. A showed so clearly, the magical fantasy of connection is a fragile one, quickly permeated with intense split-off feelings of one kind or another whenever the arrangement faces any stress, usually a situation which arouses sudden need or anger. Among the most common stressors for paranoid patients are changes in the optimal distance from the object. For example, when Ms. A. felt too close to the analyst, as in the analytic situation, or too far away from the analyst, as she did on weekends, she experienced either feelings of hostile invasion or blissful merger. The issue of character "choice," or in this paper, the "choice" of paranoid fantasies of connectedness, raises complex questions of etiology that go beyond the scope of this paper. Here the words *benign* and *malignant* refer only to manifest ideation and not to etiology or even to prognosis.

PARANOID CHARACTER AND MAGICAL CONNECTEDNESS

Focusing on the need of paranoid persons to maintain magical systems of connectedness sheds light on several aspects of paranoid psychopathology. For example, fantasies of physical connectedness (as in the connected trench fantasy) or fantasies of physical sameness, which are not the subject of this paper, are probably important in forming the unconscious homosexual fantasies so common in paranoia and of so much importance in Freud's theory. The search for connectedness through sameness, physical and mental, is also reflected in the prominent use of identification upon which paranoids rely for a feeling of connection with an object whom they know they cannot love without dangerous, potentially overwhelming ambivalence. The paranoid person always struggles with an intense identification with a hated, feared object of which he attempts to rid himself through projection and projective identification but which constantly threatens to invade and take over (Heimann, 1955).

The need for connectedness is also an important motivation in the paranoid person's use of projection. In his paper entitled, "The Mechanisms of Defense," Roy Schafer (1968) has explored the "dynamic mental content" of projection and has suggested that projection always involves an "alteration of . . . self and object representations" and "in particular, it requires a shift of content across the borders that have developed between the two types of representations (self and object)" (p. 55). In this way, projection produces a "satisfying symbiosis" through a fantasy of merger. In other words, loss of boundaries is not the unwanted side effect of projection but part of the intent of projection. Paranoids project so that they can be the same as the object, and so that they can know what the object is thinking. In this way, they ensure feeling closely connected.

Magical thoughts of connectedness involving special knowledge of the object are easy to observe in the transference in paranoid patients who assert with conviction that they know what the analyst is thinking or what the analyst is trying to do. As in identification, this demand to know what the analyst is thinking or the conviction that one already does know, is motivated by "knowledge" that the efforts to connect via loving attachments will fail.

For the paranoid, knowing the object through the intellect is always safer than attempting to know the object through empathy. In his paper "The God Complex," Ernest Jones (1913) described patients who are unable to understand other people emotionally and who resort to " 'short-cut(s)' to the knowledge of other people's minds. . . ." Such persons are fascinated by such methods as the Binet-Simon scale, the psycho-galvanic phenomenon, word-association reactions or graphology in a mechanical and literal manner, always hoping to find someone that will give results" (p. 255). His is a beautiful description of how paranoid persons gather knowledge about those to whom they cannot connect emotionally.

Schreber himself, among his many complaints about his beloved and hated God, included the fact that "God was . . . quite incapable of dealing with living men and was only accustomed to communicate with corpses" (Freud, 1911, p. 25). According to Schreber, God was completely "blinded by his ignorance of human nature"; in fact, it was "as a result of God's misunderstanding of living men [that] it was possible for Him Himself to become the instigator of the plot against Schreber" (Freud, 1911, p. 25). There may be a hint here of Schreber's awareness that if he and God are unable to make contact at the "human," or emotional level, they will have to devise other ways to connect (Freud, 1911).

Connecting through special knowledge of the object, and the special importance of knowledge, reflected in the ubiquitous need for the paranoid to know what is going on, could again be the subject of another paper. Nevertheless, one can readily observe how through subtle uses of enactment, the paranoid is, in fact, able to control and thereby to know what the analyst is thinking. This was evident in the analysis of a gifted but quietly paranoid and secretive graduate student, with a chief complaint of chronic depression and loneliness, whose dream of spaceships was reported at the beginning of this paper.

Throughout much of her long, slow analysis, Ms. B had the excruciating habit of talking very slowly and haltingly, and most aggravating to me, of almost never finishing her sentences. I developed an intense and painful countertransference feeling of being in mental chains. I was unable to associate to what Ms. B was saying as I spent so much time in the involuntary mental act of anticipating her next thought or finishing her dangling sentences. My experience of enslavement was eased somewhat when I realized that Ms. B had, in fact, managed to control the contents of my mind through the subtle maneuver of the chronic unfinished sentence. She did, in fact, always know what I was thinking for we were thinking the same thoughts at the same time. This satisfied her need to control me, but also, for the purposes of this paper, her need to feel connected to me in the face of extraordinary emotional distance.

Through projection or the *use* of projective identification, paranoids such as Ms. B assume that the analyst, in turn, controls or attempts to control the patient's thoughts, the analytic process, and ultimate result of the analysis through a program involving subtle efforts to *get* him to feel certain things, or to realize certain things about himself. The nonparanoid patient who is struggling with a frightening warded-off feeling will often claim that the analyst *wants* him to "get angry" or "feel sexually aroused"; the paranoid patient will always experience transference feelings as induced in this way by the analyst.

THE INTOLERANCE OF INDIFFFERENCE

In addition to fantasies of thinking the same thoughts and fantasies of special knowledge of the other's thoughts, the paranoid often relies simply on thinking about his object or being thought about by the object, in order to ensure feeling connected. The experience of being thought *about* by the object is most obvious in paranoid symptomatology. Indeed, when confronted with intense paranoid self-referentiality, one is often tempted to insist, "you're simply not that important"; "not everybody is thinking about you." Although some have argued that ideas of reference are secondary to paranoid megalomania (Salzman, 1960), that self-reference, above all, reflects the need to be thought about by the object and is part of the paranoid's concrete fantasy system of connectedness.

In the same vein, the paranoid cognitive style, which features scanning the environment for clues, is not simply the reflection of an innate style of thinking (Shapiro, 1965), or of an early warning system against attack. It is part of the way the paranoid uses his mind to feel connected to objects by thinking about them all the time.

As stated above, for many paranoid patients, thinking about the object and being thought about by the object are experiences which not only maintain a sense of connectedness to the object, but are, in fact, *necessary* experiences if the paranoid person is to avoid feeling totally alienated from the object world. Disconnected, withdrawn paranoid patients do not experience ideas of self-reference or conviction, but instead experience the opposite feelings of living in a frozen indifferent world peopled by strangers about whom they "haven't a clue," as in the earlier spaceship dream. Indeed, at one level, paranoid patients clearly demonstrate the effect of splitting, not so much between love and hate toward the object, but between experiences of complete indifference and total connectedness to the object.

In a recent discussion at the Association for Psychoanalytic Medicine of Kernberg's paper, "Psychopathic, Paranoid and Depressive Transferences in the Psychoanalytic Psychotherapy of Borderline Patients," Dr. Lucy La Farge (1990) suggested that splitting in borderline patients may occur not only between loving and hating attitudes toward the object, but along other lines as well. She demonstrated that a full description of different types of borderline psychopathology should consider the precise lines along which splitting occurs. She suggested that in psychopathic patients, for example, splitting occurs between "a human experience of anguish and betrayal, and an experience of self and object stripped of meaning (and truth). [The psychopath] can experience early deprivations only as meaningless losses or as evidence of catastrophic and unremitting betrayal" (personal communication). La Farge's formulations are relevant to the study of paranoid patients who can also be seen to split between experiences of meaningless alienation and experiences which are overly invested with meaning. In paranoids, however, as opposed to psychopaths, it is connectedness that loses meaning, not truthfulness. In paranoid patients, as we have tried to show, there is splitting between the experience of total indifferent detachment and the experience of total connectedness.

It is interesting to note, with regard to splitting, that in his paper, "Instincts and Their Vicissitudes," Freud (1915) remarked that "loving admits not merely of one, but of three opposites. In addition to the antithesis 'loving-hating,' there is the other one of 'loving-being loved'; and in addition to these, loving and hating taken together are the opposite of the condition of unconcern or indifference" (p. 133). In the developmental outline of object relations offered in this paper, Freud suggests that the polarity of "love-indifference" is the first to appear developmentally. Paranoid characters, because they are unable to master the polarity of love-hate, cannot rely on *feeling* connected with objects. As a result, however, the paranoid ends up having to *stay* connected to objects in the magical and concrete ways which we have outlined, or risk feeling dangerously detached. The paranoid person is so afraid of total indifference between self and object that he does not allow himself *any* experience of indifference at all toward his object. A quotient of indifference, by which we mean emotional and cognitive detachment in the service of autonomy and separateness, is a crucial component of fully developed object relations. For the paranoid, this quotient of indifference is intolerable.

What does the intolerance of indifference look like clinically? The paranoid's need to have his object thinking about him all the time is easy to observe. The wish to be thought about, especially at times of separation, is universal. Several years ago, a female psychotherapy patient (RWW), a nonparanoid college student, left her treatment for a few weeks to return home for the holidays. "I will miss you so much," she said wistfully. "I know I'll be lonely. I wish the FAA would track me during my vacation. Then at least someone would know where I am all the time." The similarity between this patient's charming fantasy of being tracked by radar and common persecutory delusions was striking. In contrast to the persecutory paranoid, however, this patient's fantasy was benign and pleasurable. It was also unaccompanied by a sense of conviction. The patient was fully able to recognize her thoughts as wishful fantasy.

A second example of the need to be thought about was provided by a patient who speculated, as patients often do, about the meaning of my taking a vacation in August. "I know that analytic institutes instruct you to take vacation in August," she said calmly. "It can't be a coincidence that all analysts go away at the same time. I understand that this is planned for the benefit of analytic patients so that they will learn to tolerate separations.'' This benign conspiracy theory, and its common variants, illustrate several aspects of magical connectedness. First of all, the separation is denied through the fantasy that the analyst's leaving is primarily motivated by her concern for her patient's developmental needs. In that sense, while superficially the analyst is off enjoying her own life, in a deeper sense, she is actually thinking mainly about her patient, and is thereby connected to her. Second, the patient is not alone in her plight but is connected by sameness to all other analytic patients who are being similarly thought about by their analysts during August and by the analytic establishment as a whole. While this fantasy was benign, the conspiracy being concocted for the patient's benefit, it was experienced with a strong sense of conviction. The patient did not recognize her thought as a wishful fantasy but as a piece of inside knowledge.

A third patient, the same Ms. A whose fantasy of my being inside her head was described above, reported another fantasy that involved my thinking about her. This fantasy was also experienced at the moment of separation. It was accompanied both by full conviction of fact as well as by hostile, persecutory ideation. ''I can tell how you feel about me when I leave the session,'' she told me one day, ''because when you are angry with me, you slam the door. You slammed the door yesterday.'' I knew this patient to be sensitive to door closings because her last memory of her father when she was 13 years old was of his closing the door as he left home, to die of a sudden myocardial infarction later that day. Reasonably certain that I did not vary significantly in my closing of the door from day to day, I raised this issue with Ms. A and wondered aloud whether she might be aware of feelings or anxieties about the separation at the end of each session that might contribute to her feelings about my behavior. While she fleetingly acknowledged wondering whether I didn't enjoy getting rid of her so I could ''think of something else,'' she became angry with my questioning her conviction, and my refusal to examine my own behavior. The following day, she was indignant and enraged. ''I know you were very angry yesterday,'' she said, ''because you really slammed the door. You were furious that I questioned your behavior.'' A difficult period ensued during which Ms. A and I spent several weeks exploring her convictions about my door closing behavior in the context of her feelings about separation and her feeling that I abandoned her at the end of each session, not only by sending her out, but by turning my attention elsewhere. In addition to what I was able to learn from Ms. A directly, I was able to observe in myself a powerful, and I think almost unavoidable countertransference response. I found that as each session ended and I went to close the door, I was so sensitized by Ms. A's volatile hypervigilance, that I was unable *not* to think about Ms. A and about how my door closing might affect her, often for some time after she had left the office. I realized that Ms. A had succeeded in partially controlling my experience at the moment of our separation, controlling it in such a way that I was, indeed, almost always thinking about her intensely both during and after the separation.

What about the necessity for the paranoid character to be, at all times, thinking about his object? This necessity, reflecting the intolerance of indifference, is fundamental to paranoid psychopathology. It is more difficult to observe than is the need to be thought about, because it is often projected, appearing in fantasies of being pursued or spied on.

What does this phenomenon look like? A quick rereading of Freud's analysis of the Schreber case (1911) reveals that Schreber's delusions reflected not only clear homosexual wishes toward the father-God, but also obvious fantasies of magical connectedness to God. Schreber expressed many fantasies of being reunited with or fused with God, as well as fantasies of being in direct contact with God through various magical pathways involving "rays" and "nerves." In Schreber's fantasy, God was unable to think of anything but him, due to the fact that "nerves of living men (such as Schreber) may exert such powerful attraction upon the nerves of God that His own existence is threatened." It is also obvious that Schreber found any evidence of God's indifference to him unbearable, referring as he did to a "glaciation due to the withdrawal of the sun." A careful reading, however, reveals a hint of Schreber's feeling that he, too, must think constantly about God, or the connection between them would be broken. Freud (1911, p. 25) describes the experience of "enforced thinking" to which (Schreber) submitted himself because he supposed that God would believe he had become an idiot and would withdraw from him if he ceased thinking for a moment. Freud attributed this "enforced thinking" to Schreber's fear of losing his reason, which like his other hypochondriacal concerns, was related to the dangers of masturbation.

40

However, one might see in Schreber's description of "enforced thinking," evidence of the intolerance of indifference that paranoids experience with regard to the object, if their connection is to be maintained. This same phenomenon was explored in the analysis of Ms. C, who was able to describe in extraordinary detail her feeling that she must think about important people in her life lest her connection to them be lost.

THE ANALYSIS OF MS. C

When Ms. C entered analysis, she was 24 years old, unemployed, and living alone. A graduate of a prestigious college, Ms. C was the second of three children from an upper-class New England WASP family. Foremost on her mind was a secret eating problem described as binging followed by vomiting, which took place twice a month for several years.

Ms. C also complained of confusion about career goals, fearing that any career choice would "swallow her up." She had worked briefly as a hospital aide but had hated the job because she was unable to say no to her bosses, and found herself thinking about her job all the time. Afraid to quit, she left her job after lying to her boss that she was going to graduate school. She was tormented by the conviction that her lie had been uncovered and that she had been blacklisted. Although Ms. C had several inventions to her name, she feared trying to market any of these lest her ideas be stolen.

Ms. C suffered from social isolation which was largely self-imposed. Although lonely, she did not want a roommate, having felt that her college roommate watched her all the time, especially when she was eating. While superficially she was popular and well liked, she avoided anything but casual contact with friends feeling self-conscious and referential in social situations. She was unable to eat in front of others, feeling certain that they monitored her intake and were contemptuous of her lack of control. At other times, she feared that friends would steal her tricks for successful dieting. She often broke off a relationship if a friend expressed ideas different from her own, in order to avoid feeling forced to "swallow" their opinions. Ms. C found solace and strength in competitive sports, at which she excelled.

Ms. C had had few and only brief romantic attachments with "boys" and dreaded trying to talk to them. In conversation, she exerted herself to be "bland and agreeable" so as not to cause any "rift." Despite her lack of involvement with men, Ms. C was preoccupied with a fantasy in which she was married to an athletic WASP with money, name, and position who she said, "would be as much like myself as possible."

Ms. C described her mother as an insecure, controlling woman determined for her daughters to succeed as debutantes, but totally unable to function as a mother of three. Ms. C described her home as dirty and messy, full of unwashed children with unplanned lives who were served meals at odd times. Ms. C's mother complained constantly that her children made life impossible with their incessant demands. She punished them by locking the refrigerator and the linen closet. She also set a timer during meals and threatened to serve uneaten food for breakfast. Enraged if the children ate food without telling her, Ms. C's mother would often go through the garbage to find out what they had been eating.

Ms. C described her physician father as laconic, with a tendency to withdraw from problems. She experienced him as alternately needy, lonely, and competitive. Ms. C loved her father and enjoyed going to the ballet and to sporting events with him.

In spite of clear paranoid concerns in her relationships with others, in sessions Ms. C was earnest, eager to work, and open about her feelings. She was relieved and grateful to have someone to talk to about loneliness, jealousy, fear, and curiosity. Anger was difficult for her to recognize, particularly toward her parents, and above all, toward me. Initially she experienced great support in a transference which she experienced as an idealized twinship. She expressed relief that I was not "Jewish like most analysts." "They are just too different." She was also pleased that in the analytic situation, I was unlikely to try to tell her what to do. Very quickly, she made a few friends, felt more in control of her eating, and got a job.

Ms. C's self-confidence improved as she began to differentiate her self-image from the image of her dysfunctional mother. At the same time, this differentiation led to loneliness as her ambivalence about autonomy and separateness became a major theme in the treatment. Ms. C spent a great deal of time in her parents' home, preoccupied herself with her parents' problems, and devoted herself to her little sister whom she felt was neglected. We explored her tendency to move home after any deepening involvement in her own life. She was afraid to develop any interests different from those of her parents lest she feel estranged, and she needed to tell her parents everything. In fact, it became clear that since childhood, she had limited her behavior to exclude everything she could *not* tell her parents.

Connected to her parents by preoccupying feelings of guilt and worry, Ms. C also maintained her connection to her parents by thinking about them all the time, and was preoccupied with whether they thought about her. Often Ms. C felt her parents had forgotten her, while at other times, she felt they were spying on her. In her sessions, she became anxious when not thinking about her parents, and she was surprised when they told her not to worry about them so much.

Indeed, Ms. C's concerns about who was thinking about whom, pervaded all important relationships. While avoiding emotional contact with friends, she kept in contact with them by thinking about them. However, she kept potential friends at bay to avoid feeling trapped into thinking about them all the time. While angry that friends never thought about her, she left her mail unanswered in defiance of having to think about friends. She felt she had always to choose between feeling "spaced out" and alone or trapped and controlled. She felt grateful to her cat who did not mind if she were indifferent. Ms. C feared entrapment not only by people but also by any potential interest, the most obvious of which was food. "If I think about food at all, I'll think about it all the time," she said. Nevertheless, when her ambivalence about involvement with others became too exhausting, Ms. C would retreat to her apartment to binge, enjoying an intense feeling of mastery in which she could take in as much as she wanted and yet still control the impact of the meal by vomiting afterward.

Ms. C projected her most primitive feelings onto her Jewish friends, who fascinated and repelled her. She saw Jews as people preoccupied with food, impulse ridden, noisy, aggressive. Although she enjoyed her sessions and was openly attached to me, her paranoid transference was projected onto a roommate with whom she shared an apartment briefly. Ms. C moved out suddenly, feeling that her roommate was intrusive and was cheating her financially.

Ms. C's happy untroubled attachment with me was disrupted suddenly when she told me she had broken off a friendship with a Jewish friend who commented that he could tell she had had garlic for dinner. She found this comment tasteless and intrusive. I suggested to Ms. C that the intrusive, tasteless Jew of whom she was thinking might also be me, as in a previous session I had commented on her choice of the words, "making a stink," when describing the expression of anger. Usually agreeable to transference comments, Ms. C was aghast. "I was not even thinking about you," she said. She became panicky and agitated; she had not been thinking of me when she thought she should have been. She reported feeling spaced out and "in another world."

From this point on, the question of how often Ms. C thought of me became a constant theme in her analysis. She became more conscious of keeping secrets from me, became convinced that I watched her for signs of secret keeping, and was certain that I could tell when she was withholding. In one extraordinary Monday session, Ms. C confessed to me that she had lied to me the previous Friday about canceling a session on Tuesday so that she could get a driver's license. In fact, she did not plan to take the test on Tuesday but was scared to tell me that she was still driving without a license. Ms. C had left the session on Friday, convinced that I could tell she was lying and had been certain all weekend that I was furious at her. In this session, she was stricken with the realization that I had *not* known she was lying. "I realize you cannot read my mind," she said through tears. "It makes me feel spaced out, like I'm floating . . . disconnected." We explored her need to have her mind read, and the symbolism of driving without a license, by which Ms. C was able to limit her sense of disconnection through her anxious preoccupation that the police were following her or trying to find her. Driving without a license served the same purpose as had lying to her bosses when she left her first job; it kept the authorities thinking about her. By the same token, she never ceased to think about these police while driving.

Sometime later, Ms. C prepared to go with her family on a week's vacation in the Caribbean, the first separation in which she was to abandon me. She had an uncharacteristic rage attack at her father because she had thoughtfully decided to pick him up at work and had ended up waiting for several hours, because he had gone home alone, thinking she was "off doing her own thing." "How would he assume that?" she raged, "when I'm never not thinking about him?" We were able to relate her rage attack to her fear that as she was looking forward to her vacation, she might be tempted not to think of me and her fear of my fury at this attack on our connection. We discussed how for her, thinking about and caring about someone were synonymous.

Following the vacation, the analysis went through a difficult period. While on vacation, Ms. C had fallen in love with a blond, athletic tennis pro with whom she had flirted briefly. She wanted to leave New York where she felt "spaced out" and unconnected and make herself part of this man's life. She became suspicious of me, convinced that I was trying to trap her in the analysis, probably because I wanted her money. She became secretive in sessions, her binging and vomiting became more intense, and she was convinced that I was scanning her face for evidence of this behavior. I interpreted to Ms. C that I was represented in both the blond tennis pro with whom she wanted to merge (she had spoken before of wanting to live with me), and in the intrusive analyst who wanted to control and exploit her. Following this interpretation, she dreamt of returning home to find her cat almost dead, because she "had not thought about it all week." I suggested that the cat represented her connection to me which she had jeopardized by not thinking about me while she was away. I reminded her that we had talked of the equation she made between "thinking about" and "caring about" prior to her leaving. Ms. C was amazed that I could even recall a session prior to her vacation, as if to confirm my suggestion that she feared our connection had been all but destroyed by her indifference.

In her panic about the destruction of our connection through her carelessness, Ms. C had attempted to repair the break with fantasies of merger with me as the tennis pro, which had in turn, led to paranoid fantasies of exploitation and control. Continued work on Ms. C's intense ambivalence over autonomy and separateness, and on the equation she made between thinking about me and meaningful connection to me, led to considerable improvement in several areas. Gradually Ms. C reported feeling both more detached, and as a result, more able to engage with others. She reported feeling both less preoccupied with thoughts about others, and less spaced out. As she gained increased freedom of thought, previously forfeited in the service of connection, she felt less need to be alone to avoid being "consumed." She reported that she was able to enjoy cooking without becoming preoccupied with food, and for the first time in her life, she did not know what food items were in her cupboards because she had not thought about it. She was amazed by her lack of vigilance in this area. Other paranoid concerns about being robbed or force fed also became less pronounced.

It is important to distinguish the kind of drastic separation problems experienced by Ms. C from separation problems ubiquitous in other kinds of analytic patients. Fears of not thinking enough about important objects are common, accompanied by a range of feared consequences in patients who may use language similar to that of Ms. C but who have very different psychopathology. It is common, for example, for masochistic patients to fear that if they don't think enough about an important object, the object will disappear or abandon them. Phobic and obsessional patients often fear that harm will come to the object if enough attention is not paid. Many neurotic patients of all types fear that to divert attention away from an important object is to risk getting involved in dangerous oedipal temptations. In these last cases, thinking about the object serves the same function as would a "wet blanket." Many patients experience all of these fears, as did Ms. C, in addition to her fear that the sense of meaningful connection could be destroyed. The blond tennis pro, after all, clearly represented an oedipal temptation.

In the case of Ms. C, as with all borderline patients, it was necessary to interpret derivatives of and defenses against primitive oral aggression and envy so that object constancy could be established and intimate relationships tolerated. Nevertheless, in this patient as in all paranoid patients, it was also necessary to interpret splitting between Ms. C's feeling that she was either completely connected to important others (as she put it, trapped and consumed) or totally "spaced out" and disconnected.

Magical and concrete fantasies of connectedness that involve the sacrifice of selfobject boundaries must always be interpreted before or along with aggression because although these fantasies are designed to avoid the problem of object inconstancy, they actually make object constancy *more* difficult to achieve. This is because these connecting fantasies involve a sacrifice of selfobject boundaries which leaves the paranoid feeling vulnerable to invasion and control. This was the case for Ms. A who felt invaded in the context of her fantasy that I could get inside her head. As a protection against invasion in the face of this dangerous imaginary permeability, many paranoid persons wear a suit of armor built out of anger and derivatives of anger (including prickliness, irritability, and outright hostility). One patient came to sessions in what she and I came to call her porcupine suit. Like a porcupine, she wore this costume of sharp barbs and prickly irritability to avoid being eaten, or consumed by positive feelings in the transference. This secondary defensive use of anger, which accounts for much of the manifest anger of the paranoid person, is the direct result of having sacrificed selfobject boundaries; it aggravates the underlying problem of object inconstancy as does any increase in anger toward the object. In this way, a vicious cycle is set up whereby the problem of object inconstancy is handled by establishing systems of connectedness which sacrifice selfobject boundaries; rage is then used defensively to protect the boundaries of the self and the resulting increase in rage aggravates the problem of object inconstancy.

Fantasies of magical connectedness involving the sacrifice of self and object boundaries are often expressed in the language of body experiences such as "invasion," "penetration," being "emptied out," or being "swallowed up." Although this prominent use of body symbolism invites interpretation of libidinal and aggressive drive derivatives, this paper emphasizes that such fantasies *also* represent disturbed attempts at attachment which must be interpreted first. If paranoid fantasies of connectedness are attacked suddenly, for example, if the analyst challenges the paranoid sense of conviction without taking its purpose into account, the patient will become suspicious and angry. However, if the need to feel magically connected, the corresponding fear of utter indifference, and the high price paid for this split, are interpreted over time, particularly during periods of relative calmness, the possibility of establishing object constancy is greatly increased. As in the case of Ms. C, when the freedom which accompanies a quotient of indifference was restored, the affective components of object relations became easier to manage. When selfobject boundaries have been sacrificed, even in the service of a desired connectedness, anger becomes terrifying, and love feels like a coercive trap. Only the freedom of separateness, reflected in the possibility of a bit of indifference, makes real love possible.

REFERENCES

Blum, H. P. (1980), Paranoia and beating fantasy: An inquiry into the psychoanalytic theory of paranoia. *J. Amer. Psychoanal. Assn.*, 28:331–361.

——— (1981), Object inconstancy and paranoid conspiracy. *J. Amer. Psychoanal. Assn.*, 29:789–813.

Freud, S. (1911), Psycho-analytic notes on an autobiographical account of a case of paranoia (dementia paranoides). *Standard Edition*, 12:3–84. London: Hogarth Press, 1958.

——— (1915), Instincts and their vicissitudes. *Standard Edition*, 14:109–140. London: Hogarth Press, 1957.

Fussell, P. (1975), *The Great War and Modern Memory*. London: Oxford University Press.

Heimann, P. (1955), A combination of defense mechanisms in paranoid states. In: *New Directions in Psychoanalysis*, ed. M. Klein, P. Heimann, & R. E. Money-Kyrle. New York: Basic Books, pp. 240–265.

Jacobson, E. (1964), *The Self and Object World*. New York: International Universities Press.

Jones, E. (1913), The God complex. In: *Essays in Applied Psychoanalysis*, Vol. 2. New York: International Universities Press, 1964, pp. 244–265.

Kernberg, O. F. (1970a), A psychoanalytic classification of character pathology. *J. Amer. Psychoanal. Assn.*, 18:800–822.

——— (1970b), Treatment of the narcissistic personality. In: *Borderline Conditions and Pathological Narcissism*. New York: Jason Aronson, 1975, pp. 227–262.

Klein, M. (1946), Notes on some schizoid mechanisms. *Internat. J. Psycho-Anal.*, 27:99–110.

Knight, R. P. (1940), The relationship of latent homosexuality to the mechanisms of paranoid delusions. *Bull. Menninger Clinic*, 4:149–159.

La Farge, L. (1990), Discussion of "Psychopathic, paranoid and depressive transferences in the psychodynamic psychotherapy of borderline patients" by Otto F. Kernberg, Association for Psychoanalytic Medicine, October 2, 1990. *Bull. Assn. Psychoanal. Med.*, 31:36–44.

Panel (1968), Panel discussion. *Internat. J. Psycho-Anal.*, 49:506–512.

Salzman, L. (1960), Paranoid state-theory and therapy. *Arch. Gen. Psychiatry*, 2:101–115.

Schafer, R. (1968), The mechanisms of defense. *Internat. J. Psycho-Anal.*, 49:49–62.

Shapiro, D. (1965), *Neurotic Styles*. New York: Basic Books.

4

Paranoia from a Characterological Standpoint

David Shapiro, Ph.D.

Some years ago I proposed certain revisions of the classical theory of paranoia in an effort to correct that theory's generally acknowledged deficiencies, as well as certain deficiencies that are not so generally acknowledged (Shapiro, 1965, pp. 54–107; 1981, pp. 134–173). I would like to summarize these deficiencies and restate my revisions as concisely as I can.

In the classical theory, paranoia, at least in the male case, to which I will limit most of this presentation, is understood as a defense against abhorrent unconscious homosexual wishes (Freud, 1911). The theory, I believe, contains a powerful and essential part and a much weaker but, also, less essential part. I want to consider these two parts separately.

The powerful and essential part of the theory consists, first, of the discovery of the abhorrent and threatening homosexual wish. Second, it consists of the inference that conscious awareness of this wish is forestalled by the relocation of the threat to an external arena—its transformation, in other words, into paranoia. This discovery that, in the male at least, the abhorrence of an unconscious homosexual wish is the driving force of paranoia, has been described by Robert Knight

(1940), as perhaps the most generally accepted and widely confirmed psychoanalytic theory of psychosis. Whether it will turn out that such an abhorrence is present in every case of male paranoia is an important question but not critical to the value of the discovery. It is certainly not difficult to find confirming cases and in the case of Schreber, whose memoir Freud used to develop his theory, the evidence for such an abhorrence is clear.

But there is a far less convincing part of the theory: it is the account of the processes through which this subjective transformation from an internal to an external conflict is accomplished. The well-known formula is as follows: the homosexual wish represented in, "I love him," is repudiated and denied with the idea, "I hate him"; this idea is, in turn, projectively transformed into "he hates me," which justifies the addendum, "I hate him because he hates me."

This cumbersome formula seems to me an ad hoc construction, unexplained by any familiar, general psychological processes. In particular, the central mechanism of paranoid projection, and thus the critical step from "I hate him" to "he hates me," is not made clear in its workings. The conception of projection simply as an "expulsion" of unacceptable feelings or ideas (in some way derived from the physical act of expelling waste or spitting out what is distasteful) is not satisfactory. Even if a process of this kind were made psychologically understandable, it would seem able to account at best for the idea, "*He* hates," comparable to what has been proposed for the case of male jealousy, "It is *she* who loves him, not I." But it would not in any obvious way be able to account for the essential idea, "He hates *me*." In short, the situation as far as the classical theory is concerned seems to me to be this: it has shown us convincingly that an internal conflict of a particular kind is, for anxiety-dispelling purposes, that is, purposes of defense, transformed into a conflict that is experienced as external; but it has not shown us, in an equally convincing way, how this takes place.

Apart from this problem of the workings of the defense process, there are at least two other questions which were left without satisfactory answers by the theory: First, why this particular defense process? Why not, say, repression? This question of the so-called "choice of neurosis," was raised by Freud himself in his 1911 paper, but left unanswered. Its answer was not to be found within the libido theory alone; the problem involves additional constituents of the personality.

The point applies equally to a further question, raised by Knight (1940): Why such an intense abhorrence by these people of the homosexual wish, anyway? It seems apparent that all these problems—the explanation of the externalization process, the problem of the "choice" of defense, and the intensity of the abhorrence of the homosexual wish itself—required for their solution a more complete understanding of the workings of the ego in paranoia. Or, in more general psychological language, they required a more complete understanding of the nature and workings of paranoid character or personality.

It is possible now, particularly with the accumulated data of diagnostic psychological tests, to consider certain general features of paranoid character as known. I am speaking of certain attitudes, ways of thinking, and forms of experience. These features may be summarized as the expressions of a severe variety of rigid character. I want now to give a general picture of this character and to show that it can provide answers to the questions I have indicated.

I would like to introduce that picture in a particular way, which may seem somewhat indirect. I want to take as a starting point the relation of paranoid character to the less severe form of rigid character in obsessive–compulsive conditions. The reason for the comparative approach is this: We are concerned here with the transformation of an internal conflict into one that is experienced as external; and this is precisely the transformation that can be studied in the comparison of the relatively less rigid obsessive–compulsive character with the more severely rigid paranoid character.

The kinship between obsessive–compulsive and paranoid conditions is a familiar one clinically as well as theoretically. In many respects, the two conditions have a similar "feel." Paranoid fanaticism, for example, can easily be described as a more passionate and intense, and, of course, even less influenceable, kind of dogmatism; paranoid suspicious bias resembles the kind of obsessive concern that finds its object everywhere; and the paranoid delusion, itself, in its general quality as an anxious, preoccupying idea stripped of realistic proportion, may resemble an extreme form of obsession. In certain cases the differential diagnosis between severe obsessional and paranoid conditions can be difficult to establish; and the personality from which an acute paranoid condition emerges is frequently a severely obsessive or compulsive one. Altogether, the formal relation between the two conditions, regarded as two varieties and two degrees of severity of rigid style, is strong.

The meaning of "rigid" as it applies to obsessive and compulsive conditions is quite specific. It refers, first, to the undeviating, willful purposefulness and deliberateness characteristic of them, a constant purposefulness that also has the effect of narrowing the range of conscious subjective experience, particularly emotional experience. But the term "rigid" also refers to the special kind of conscientiousness that underlies that purposefulness and deliberateness. This conscientiousness involves living with a more or less constant and oppressive awareness of subjectively authoritative, obligatory, often moralistic rules and imperatives. It typically involves, also, an anxious kind of emulation of certain models, a continual reference to these figures as authoritative standards, and a continual measurement of the self according to them. The person who lives in this way lives with a constant sensation of "should," not only of what he "should" *do* but, also, of what he "should" *be,* and he reflexively makes an effort to be that. Hence, his behavior is stilted and, inasmuch as he thinks he should be something more than he is, often pompous. His judgment is often correspondingly dogmatic and full of borrowed authority. In all this, however, a consciousness of not being enough, of not being what one should be, or, worse, being what one should not be, is never eliminated. There are constant struggles with the self against "laziness," or various other kinds of "giving in" to oneself—what is experienced as "weakness." These are struggles of will. Essentially, they are struggles against the temptation to do what one *wants* to do—unrecognized as such—instead of what one *should* do. Success in such struggles is called "willpower." All this is part of the effort to identify with, and to assert over oneself, an authority which does not feel genuinely one's own.

In the case of paranoia, it is this struggle with oneself which is transformed into an experience of conflict with an external antagonist. The correspondence is quite exact. Where the compulsive person experiences a conscious struggle against giving in to himself and against various kinds of weakness of will, the paranoid person experiences a struggle against external efforts to subjugate or coerce him, or to weaken his will, make him give in or undermine his resistance in various other ways. Where the compulsive person contends with feelings that he is not what he should be, the paranoid person contends with external efforts to humiliate him and make him feel small. This transformation from an experience of internal conflict to one of external conflict obviously includes a more complete subjective estrangement from certain aspects of the self, such as temptations that might constitute "weakness," and from certain feelings about the self, such as feelings of shame and inferiority. It is my proposal that this transformation and self-estrangement can be understood as effects of a more severe rigidity of the sort I have described.

Imagine such a condition of a more rigid will or self-direction than the case of the obsessive-compulsive. This is a condition, in other words, in which the identification of the self with authoritative standards and images of what one should be is more rigid, more deliberate, and purposeful than in the compulsive case. It is a condition, therefore, in which the range of emotional experience is narrowed further and in which the reflexive avoidance of "weakness," and the reflexive effort to dispel feelings that one is not what one should be, that is, feelings of shame and inferiority, are more extreme. One is imagining, then, an individual more stilted and artificial in his behavior, perhaps no longer merely pompous and dogmatic, but grandiose. It is an individual more completely cut off from the actuality of himself and his feelings—the patient, Schreber, for example, referred to himself as "morally unblemished."

When I speak here about will or self-direction, I am speaking about autonomy; and autonomy has both an internal and an external aspect. Individuals of rigid and uncertain autonomy or self-direction must guard two fronts: they must guard against "weakness" in the sense of giving in to themselves, and, also, in the sense of giving in to others. Everyone is familiar with the stubbornness of compulsive people, the difficulty of influencing them. But on the whole compulsive people are wrapped up in themselves, driving themselves in their work, measuring their insufficiencies, and consciously wrestling with their weaknesses. In all this, they may even be quite imperturbable from the outside. But when one imagines the more severely rigid person, say the grandiose person, who is cut off from and cannot tolerate conscious awareness of weakness, or of feelings of inferiority and shame, the picture changes from stubbornness and imperturbability to defensive sensitivity.

The reason is not hard to see. However unaware that person may be of such feelings of weakness, inferiority, or shame, these feelings will be exacerbated by a variety of external circumstances. Any treatment at the hands of another person that may seem coercive or disrespectful—anything that resembles being "pushed around," a rebuff or other insult or indignity, particularly from a person of superior rank; sometimes the mere presence of figures who are respected, often grudgingly respected—any such circumstance will threaten to remind that grandiose person of his smallness, that is, will humiliate him. Respected figures, admired figures, superiors, will therefore regularly become objects of prideful, defensive sensitivity and antagonism.

I am proposing that a defensive and antagonistic relationship to the external world or, at least, to certain kinds of figures in it, is intrinsic to the severely rigid character and is independent of and prior to projection. In other words, the workings of such character at the same time cuts off the individual from conscious awareness of his own feelings of shame and weakness and replaces that self-awareness with a defensive concern with external figures who excite unrecognized sensations of shame and weakness. The locus of concern is thereby shifted from what is internal to what is external. This defensive and antagonistic relationship is not characterized merely by an unspecific aggression, but by the sensitivity, the alertness to humiliation, the bitterness, and ultimately the hatred that the prideful inferior or subordinate harbors toward his grudgingly admired betters. Furthermore, this defensive sensitivity and antagonism toward external figures will be exacerbated by any intensification of unrecognized internal sensations of shame or weakness. Thus, the comparatively simple dynamics of the severely rigid character's defensiveness is the pivot of the transformation of an internal tension into one that is experienced as external.

This, of course, is not yet projection; that further step remains, but it is not a difficult step. If the already rigid and defensive man feels weaker and more ashamed, without recognizing that he feels so, he becomes more defensive. He becomes more purposefully and anxiously mobilized and alert, still further cut off from his own feelings, and even more rigidly biased in his judgments and perceptions. Such a person cannot afford the luxury of open-mindedness or balanced judgment; he searches only for signs of threat, not for an absence of such signs. To be more exact, the judgments of such a person come less to resemble active judgments and come more to be the immediate, too eager reactions of a fixed unrecognized bias to anything that can satisfy that bias, regardless of its mitigating context.

The nature of the identified external threat, however, will not be a simple reproduction of a repudiated impulse or feeling. The external threat will be a defensive transformation of the internal threat. Specifically, the projective threat will be an experience of threat or insult to the autonomy or the will, the authority, dignity, or self-respect of the paranoid person. In other words, the projective threat will be constructed, not simply out of repudiated impulses and feelings but out of the particular anxieties generated in the rigid person by repudiated impulses and feelings. Altogether, therefore, we reverse the usual understanding: instead of saying that paranoid defensiveness is the product of projection, we say that the projective process is the outcome of the rigid character's defensive mobilization.

Generally speaking, the projective threat is likely to take either of two forms. The less severe and probably more common form is a simple product of defensiveness; an anticipation or suspicion, particularly in the presence of figures of authority or superior rank, of humiliating criticism or disrespect. This is commonly described as superego projection. The more severe form of projection typically involves a coercive threat or an experience of actual coercion, such as a threat of sexual subjugation, as in Schreber's case, or an experience of external control, as by an influencing machine, or some type of external disabling or weakening of will, such as a mysterious weakening of the will to resist sexual subjugation.

I would like now to turn to the other question I referred to initially: Why should the homosexual wish, in particular, incite such an anxiety and defensive mobilization? Why such an abhorrence and dread of homosexuality in these individuals—in Schreber, for instance? It would be easy to say that such an abhorrence is only an expectable expression of the moralism and the respect for conventional authority common to rigid character. Such an answer, I think, would not be sufficient to explain the intensity of this reaction. There is a deeper answer which is exemplified in the Schreber case itself. The abhorrence and dread of the homosexual wish from Schreber's point of view was not merely an abhorrence of a particular object, or kind, of sexual impulse. It was not even a dread—though this comes closer—of transformation from a male into a female. It was specifically a dread of a transformation from an upright, "morally unblemished," ascetic and rigidly dutiful man, who prided himself on his manly honor, into a "harlot"; not merely a female but a degraded and wanton female suffused by what he called "voluptuousness" (Schreber, 1903). This was the morally unblemished Schreber's idea of female sexuality. It was an idea of sexual subjugation and surrender, a masochistic sexuality essentially, an idea of a loss or an abandonment of all self-control, all morality, dignity, and will, to an erotic debasement and humiliation. The idea of such a sexuality and such an identity is abhorrent and dreadful to him not merely because its sexual object is improper but because it is an idea and an experience of the self which is inimical and intolerable to his whole character, his whole "way of being," to use an old phrase of Wilhelm Reich's.

There is yet another question, also raised by Knight (1940), concerning the relation of homosexuality and male paranoia: What is the basis of the strong homosexual wish in these cases in the first place? We cannot exclude a biological factor in such a wish, but we can perceive some characterological basis for it, at least of an indirect sort. For there is another side to this image of masochistic female sexuality that is so abhorrent to the rigid male. It is just such a sexual image, an image of sexual subjugation and debasement, that will, also, be most intensely erotic to him. It will be so precisely because it contains the condition of "giving in," of a surrender, an enforced divestment, of all the constraints of the rigid and moralistic will. Thus, the questions, why is the idea of sexual femaleness so abhorrent to the rigid male, and, why is the homosexual wish so powerful in him, turn out to have the same answer.

I would like to add one addendum to what I have said; it concerns paranoia in the female. If this understanding is correct, a homosexual wish will not play the same role in female paranoia that it plays in the male case. It is more likely that the idea of a heterosexual masochistic sexual subjugation will play the corresponding role in the female rigid character, and, for her, will be both intensely erotic and deeply abhorrent.

REFERENCES

Freud, S. (1911), Psycho-analytical notes upon an autobiographical account of a case of paranoia (dementia paranoides). *Standard Edition*, 12:3–79. London: Hogarth Press, 1958.

Knight, R. P. (1940), The relationship of latent homosexuality to the mechanism of paranoid delusions. *Bull. Menninger Clinic*, 4: 149–159.

Schreber, D. P. (1903), *Memoirs of My Nervous Illness*. London: William Dawson, 1955.

Shapiro, D. (1965), *Neurotic Styles*. New York: Basic Books.

———— (1981), *Autonomy and Rigid Character*. New York: Basic Books.

Part II

Paranoia in Organizational and Social Systems

5

Leadership Styles and Organizational Paranoiagenesis

Otto F. Kernberg, M.D.

In an earlier contribution (Kernberg, 1993), starting from Elliott Jaques's (1976) concept of requisite and paranoiagenic social organizations, I concluded that there are powerful paranoiagenic forces at work in all social organizations and that these are responsible for widespread pathological behavior in members of such institutions ranging from the antisocial, at one extreme, to the paranoid in the middle range, to the depressive and excessively self-critical at the other extreme. I concluded that the causes of organizational paranoiagenesis resided in (1) the breakdown of the task systems of organizations when their primary tasks become irrelevant or overwhelming or are paralyzed by unforeseen, undiagnosed, or mishandled constraints; (2) the activation of regressive group processes when the institution is malfunctioning; (3) the latent predisposition to paranoid regression that is a universal characteristic of individual psychology.

In that earlier work, I pointed to faulty organizational leadership as a major cause of the breakdown of task performance, and proposed that, although faulty leadership may be owing to the personality characteristics of leaders in key administrative positions, all breakdowns in organizational functioning initially look as if the personalities of key leaders were responsible; only a careful analysis of the organization will differentiate those cases in which the leader's pathological personality is actually the cause of the organizational breakdown from those in which it is only a presenting symptom. I referred to frequent causes of regression in organizational group processes such as political action in the organization that is tangential or unrelated to functional institutional goals, faulty distribution of authority (either an excess or a lack of adequate power invested in the legitimate authorities), and incompetent leaders.

Elsewhere (Kernberg, 1991) I described five desirable personality characteristics for organizational leaders: (1) high intelligence; (2) personal honesty and imperviousness to the political process; (3) a capacity for establishing and maintaining object relations in depth; (4) a healthy degree of narcissism; (5) a healthy, justifiable anticipatory paranoid attitude (in contrast to naiveté). I pointed to the paranoiagenic effects of the ascendance in leadership positions of persons with strong paranoid, narcissistic, or antisocial characteristics, but also suggested that such ascendance may sometimes also be secondary to the degree of regression of the group processes in the organization. The degree of prominence of paranoid individuals in the group process at any particular time may be considered an indirect indicator of the extent to which paranoiagenesis prevails in the organization.

This brief review is offered in order to provide the background and context for a further exploration of the effects of the leader's personality on increasing or decreasing paranoiagenesis in the institution. I have become impressed in recent years by the extent to which, regardless of the challenges posed to institutions by external reality, and even by the development of crises affecting the very existence of an institution, the quality of leadership may be crucial in permitting the organization to survive and to function without a severe paranoiagenic regression. Indeed, sometimes what looks like an institution with clear and viable tasks with a task-oriented organizational structure may suffer from severe paranoiagenesis derived from the characteristics of its leadership. In earlier work (Kernberg, 1979), I pointed to the negative consequences of excessively narcissistic, paranoid, obsessive, and schizoid traits in the personality of the leader, with particular emphasis on the negative effects of pathological narcissism on the leader's immediate entourage and the organization as a whole. Here I shall elaborate on that subject, focusing on certain pathological leadership styles and their effects on the organization.

While positive bonds among the members of an organization depend on their mutual identifications with a common task ("task systems") and on identification with their particular professional group ("sentient system" [Rice, 1965]), such libidinal ties also are dependent upon the members' dependency on and admiration of their leader (Freud, 1921). At the same time, insofar as all human relationships are ambivalent, and members of an organization are particularly susceptible to rivalries because of professional advancement and administrative hierarchies, the potential for aggression also becomes important in the organization's social life. In addition, together with idealizing and depending on leadership, the individual members' preoedipal and oedipal conflicts with parental authority, ordinarily submerged and controlled by the reality of the common task (the "work group" [Bion, 1961]) become activated in institutional life.

These subtle undercurrents of libidinal and aggressive strivings among the members of the organization are intensified by the activation of regressive group processes, that is, the activation of the basic group assumptions of "fight–flight" and "dependency" described by Bion (1961), and the generalized fear of aggression characteristic of large-group processes described by Turquet (1975). The aggression mobilized by these regressive group processes is controlled by defensive operations, including their general unconscious displacement of aggression onto the organizational "gate-keepers," namely, those who control entrance to the organization, adherence to rules and regulations, hiring, firing, and promotion procedures. Thus, aggression is displaced and projected onto the organizational leadership at all levels; and as part of this aggression, so is repressed or dissociated sadism.

A jointly generated ideology reflecting the idealization of the institutional tasks and what often amounts to a mythology of such institutional tasks (a commonly shared fantasy about the institution's purpose and importance) also become charged with aggressive as well as libidinal investment. Legally vested authority in the organization's leadership is reinforced by the power stemming from the authority delegated to them by members of the institution and by the strivings for power residing in the leaders' own personalities. Thus real and projected aggression crystalize in the organization's administrative structures and are conducted "upward" to the top leadership.

When socially determined excess of power is vested in the leadership, or a historically determined excessive power vested in the leadership transforms functional authority into authoritarian power, the conditions are ripe for potential misuse of such power in the discharge of surplus aggression, with a paranoiagenic effect on the future organization. Now the personality of the leader becomes crucial in managing that excessive, potentially dangerous and explosive, but potentially also creative and work-protective use of power, and the discharge of its implicit aggression.

The location of power vested in the institution's leadership is not stable. It may be incremented or decreased with fluctuating delegations of authority from outside the institution onto top leadership; adequacy or inadequacy of the organizational structure to the task; the delegated authority from all the members of the institution in terms of their confidence and idealization (versus distrust and devaluation) of their leadership; the rigidity or chaos of the institution's bureaucratic arrangements; and, of course, the leader's management of his power and authority.

The organizational leader stands at the crossroad of powerful aggressive forces impinging upon his functioning. They include his internal aggressive strivings, his ability to sublimate his aggression in his leadership tasks, the effort to resist against the aggression being projected onto him, and his ability to carry out decision-making under conditions of uncertainty. At the same time, the loneliness of the leadership function, the necessary frustration of the leader's dependency needs, the unconscious oedipal, sexualized temptations the organization confronts him with, the seduction into "justified indignation" giving vent to dissociated sadism of his own—all operate upon the leader in the direction of stimulating the activation and discharge of aggression onto the institution. Unresolved unconscious conflicts and personality structures of various kinds enter in collusion with these temptations.

In complementary fashion, the expression of aggression on the part of the leader is immediately amplified by his authority, by the influence he exerts over group processes in the organization, and by the direct control of task systems, groups, and individuals that he may exercise. Such direct control over others fosters the activation of primitive defensive operations in the leader, particularly of projective identification. Paradoxically, the leader is in a position vis-à-vis his subordinates comparable to that of the patient to his psychotherapist. The subordinates' task is to understand the messages from the leader and to utilize them for task performance, just as the psychotherapist is open to messages from the patient in order to carry out his psychotherapeutic task. The patient's projective identification powerfully influences the therapist's countertransference; the leader's projective identification has a strong influence on the attitudes of his subordinates.

Under optimal circumstances, these projective processes are controlled by the leader's orientation to the task, his intelligence, security, moral integrity, the respect for his subordinates, and the libidinal investment in them as part of the joint dedication to the task. The leader's sense of security helps him tolerate the unavoidable ambivalence of his subordinates in their organizational functioning.

Under pathological circumstances, projective mechanisms are exaggerated, amplified in their effects because of the concentration of power invested in the leader's authority, and "self-fulfilling prophecies" distort the leader's interpersonal relations in the organization as the administrative structure is affected by his actions. The most general dynamic involved here includes the projection of his internal world of object relations on the surrounding organizational environment. Idealized and persecutory object representations, realistic, idealized, and devalued self representations are projected onto his psychosocial environment, and the intrapsychic relationships to his internalized object world are played out unconsciously in the interpersonal world of the organization. In other words, the leader treats his staff as internal objects, and/or induces in them the attitudes of his repressed and dissociated, projected self and object representations. The more pathological his internal world of object relations, the more it is played out in the interpersonal world of the organization. Let us consider some typical examples.

THE LEADER WHO CANNOT SAY NO

I begin with this example because, although on the surface, this type of leadership would seem diametrically opposite to the kind that ordinarily would increase paranoiagenesis in the institution, the effect of this leadership style is in fact paranoiagenic. Various types of personality style may foster the incapacity to take a firm, determined stance. Narcissistic personalities who need to be loved by everybody and wish to avoid frustrating those by whom they wish to be loved; or narcissistic personalities with enormous internal pressure to "feed" everybody because of the projection of their dependency needs onto the members of the organization; dependent–infantile personalities who hope that gratifying their co-workers will, in turn, promote these co-workers' efforts to gratify them—all are personality qualities contributing to the incapacity to take a stand.

At a different level, fear of the consequences of their own aggression may promote such compliant behavior. A more complex underlying dynamic is presented by some leaders whose reaction formation against intense sadistic needs is played out in a friendliness of manner. They simultaneously attempt to agree with everybody, but, unconsciously, are thus intensifying the competition among them, and fostering a paranoid atmosphere at one tier below their own. They may seem most agreeable, but those who work immediately with them experience them as friendly but disconcerting and are left with a sense of uncertainty about what is expected from them.

Subordinates of such leaders often find themselves in the middle of conflict with others in parallel functions while the leader maintains himself carefully at a distance and emerges as well intentioned (but not too helpful). Sometimes strong paranoid developments may occur two levels below the leader who, unconsciously, has really engineered the conflict. His attitude of puzzled and fascinated "unhappiness" over the "senseless fights" among his subordinates may betray the underlying repressed and dissociated sadism.

There are, of course, instances of somebody being promoted to a position for which he is simply not qualified. Such a leader expresses his uncertainty by a wish to keep in the good graces of his subordinates, an incapacity to live up to the role demands of his position, a lack of conceptual clarity, a tendency to get lost in details or paralyzed by tasks, with a corresponding tendency to excessive delegation of authority and a lack of clarity in the contradictory nature of his delegation to various members of his team. The incompetent leader who cannot say no, however, induces a sense of chaos and frustration rather than suspicion in those who are depending on him. The leader whose unconscious sadism is expressed in contention among subordinates, in contrast, tends to be protected, for a long time, from the organization's awareness of the true locus of origin of the conflicts.

The leader who cannot say no responds positively, of course, to the last person with whom he talks, and conflicts among subordinates may derive from contradictory conclusions of these subordinates. This does not apply to the leader whose support of his subordinates contains the unconscious seeds of conflicts among them and where a much greater subtlety obscures the contradictory messages given.

Another, more pathological variant of this constellation is presented by the leader who consciously attempts to manipulate his subordinates by the principle of divide and rule, a sign that narcissistic pathology with antisocial tendencies is in the foreground. The avoidance of open conflicts represents a defense against the expression of direct aggression in organizational interchange, an effort to avoid overtly making enemies while attempting to maintain control. The result is a decrease of mutual trust throughout the entire system, leading to paranoid developments. Major institutional mismanagement and administrative scandals may erupt from the apparently harmonious surface of interaction created by this type of leadership.

THE LEADER WHO HAS TO BE ADMIRED AND LOVED

This pattern reflects the psychopathology of the narcissistic personality in a leadership position, to which I have referred in earlier work (1979). Leaders with narcissistic personalities show strong exhibitionistic tendencies, make it very clear to their subordinates that they need to be loved and admired, have great difficulty accepting criticism from subordinates, and rapidly tend to distort administrative structures into an inner circle of sycophantic favorites, and an outer, rejected group of disgruntled, disappointed, resentful, and suspect "enemies." This type of leader can be very direct and certain and may accept advice from those he feels sure are admiring subordinates, but because of his intolerance of criticism he may not get necessary feedback regarding institutional problems.

In the long run, the lack of the capacity for assessing individuals in depth that is typical for the psychopathology of narcissism may bring about a deterioration in the leadership quality throughout middle management levels and add to the organizational damage. Although narcissistic leaders are often charismatic, it is important not to confuse these two characteristics: a leader with great conceptual skills, plenty of energy and enthusiasm, and an aggressive pursuit of goals who, at the same time, possesses a strong capacity for investment in depth in others may provide charismatic leadership without the negative side effects of the narcissistic personality.

Although the leaders who cannot say no and those who need to be admired and loved may look like ''consensus'' leaders, consensus leadership may also be provided by a completely different personality style, namely, that of a leader committed to a functional, team-oriented leadership that is strong and decisive without imposing his personality on the group. To the contrary, the leader who is self-confident may find it easier to delegate leadership, under specific circumstances, to other members of the organization more prepared than he is to deal with certain problems.

The narcissistic leader's lack of capacity to listen to what is not harmonious with his own views, the need to defend himself against his own intense unconscious envy, make the position of his most creative co-workers very difficult. It is not enough to admire him, it is important that conscious envious feelings not be stirred up in him. The unconscious (or conscious) awareness of these dynamics within his inner circle tends to transform the most capable co-workers into passive acquiescence, and a circular reaction is created within which it seems as if original thinking and decision making were located exclusively in the leader. Furthermore, his devaluation of those who are not his admirers and whose productivity he unconsciously envies may inhibit the development of creativity in other areas of the institution. Typically, narcissistic leaders find it easier to hire valuable persons from outside the institution rather than to promote from inside, thereby inhibiting organizational development. In educational institutions, these are highly admired teachers who may develop young students but not senior faculty.

THE LEADER WHO HAS TO BE IN TOTAL CONTROL

This leadership style corresponds to a traditional authoritarian leadership that should be differentiated from an objective need to carry out adequate boundary control of the institution, to set goals and implement them, and to be really in charge. What I am referring to here is a leadership style wherein the exercise of control becomes an objective for its own purpose, typically reflected in micromanagement, suspiciousness, and resentment when decisions are made without the leader's knowledge or approval, and all processes throughout the organization have to undergo nonfunctional "loops" to assure support from the top, even before a proposal is worked out at a local level.

Various types of personality difficulties may converge into this leadership style. Some narcissistic personalities need to be not only admired and loved but also scrupulously obeyed to prevent the emergence, as the leader sees it, of potential enemies. Narcissistic personalities with strong paranoid features tend to develop such a leadership style. Some leaders with strong paranoid tendencies may express, through the need to control, their suspicious nature, the sense that they have to constantly protect themselves against manipulation, cheating, and betrayal.

If the underlying pathology of the need for excessive control is predominantly narcissistic, it also may reflect the leader's unconscious fears of being left out, of failure and incompetence if he is not in charge; in other words, the need to defend an idealized self-concept and to avoid the emergence of a devalued one. And, insofar as the narcissistic leader projects his devalued self and object representations onto his subordinates, the unconscious devaluation of those who work with him may have devastating effects on their creativity and self-esteem. The development of the depressive and excessive self-critical attitude I have described elsewhere is a typical consequence of paranoiagenesis within the healthier spectrum of the members of the institution (Kernberg, 1993).

Some obsessive–compulsive personalities have to carry out complete control in order to avoid a feared situation of "chaos," and as a direct expression of striving for sadistic power. In more inhibited obsessive personalities, the need to be in control may exist in association with indecisiveness, so that organizational functioning is dramatically slowed down. Here, however, I am describing a style that is excessively controlling but decisive at the same time.

When obsessive–compulsive tendencies in the leader dominate, there exists a strong capacity for establishing object relations in depth, a realistic assessment of those with whom he works, and the need to carry out control is not accompanied by the inordinate need to be loved and admired, as with the narcissistic personality. If the leader has unusual intellectual, creative, and moral qualities, the tendency toward excessive exercise of control may be compensated by this very efficiency; this may be an ideal leadership style when "turbulence" exists in the external environment, or rapid organizational change, or a crisis situation. For a stable organization, however, the long-term effects of this leadership style may still be significantly paranoiagenic and, in this regard, diminish organizational efficiency.

If the underlying dynamics are predominantly paranoid, the leader who needs to carry out excessive control typically presents projective mechanisms, the need for omnipotent control as a complement to projective identification, the division of the world into friends and enemies, and, particularly, the definition of individuals or areas of the organization as hostile, with a corresponding challenging hostility in reaction to those hostile forces, and a generalized hyperalertness and suspiciousness in his organizational dealings. Here the mutual reinforcement of paranoid features in the leadership, a consequent group regression, and reinforcement of paranoiagenesis in the institution, which in turn further strengthens the paranoid elements in the leadership, is the rule. In the organization's group processes, typically the leader may attack one or several of his subordinates who submit meekly to these attacks. A silent majority seems to condone the leader's attack, while the reactions among the other members of the management group may be gleeful ("I am glad I did not catch it today") or depressed (expressing the unconscious feelings of guilt for abandoning their colleague or colleagues).

In the long run, an excessively controlling organizational leadership may have exhausting effects on intermediate levels of management, for an enormous amount of energy must go into reassuring the leader's control and into negotiating the organization's functional needs in compromises with the leader's demands. Intuitively, leaders at an intermediate level attempt to protect their junior workers from the effects of excessive control at the top, but an atmosphere of caution and conservatism permeates the entire organization.

A frequent complication is the gradual gathering, at an intermediate level, of individuals with strongly narcissistic features, able to adjust to excessive control on the top while maintaining an internal distance that protects them from the organization's paranoid regression, "narcissistically floating," one might say, in an organizational structure to which they adjust without a deep commitment. Such developments may lead to an association between the paranoid narcissistic leader and a lieutenant with antisocial features as instruments for institutional control (the relationship between Stalin and Beria is a typical example).

THE ABSENTEE LEADER

The paranoiagenic effects of absentee leadership derive from the lack of availability, whenever group regressions occur, of task-oriented maintenance or reorganization of task systems and task boundaries, of corrective feedback, and of the neutralization of rumors by authoritative information and directives from the top. Insofar as absentee leadership weakens administrative structures and may result in chaos, group regression and authoritarianism tend to coexist. If the organization is relatively stable, if its products have an assured market, and if the external environment is stable, the underlying problems may last for many years. But absentee leadership may be the prelude to organizational breakdown in times of acute environmental change or crisis.

Various types of personality difficulties may be responsible for absentee leadership: a leader with schizoid personality can exert leadership through written directives to a small select group but is extremely reluctant to interact directly with his entire staff. Or the leader has been promoted beyond his technical expertise or interest and is occupying his position for other reasons—financial support, for example, or political influence. Or a very narcissistic individual is more interested in the prestige provided by the position than in any investment in the organization's goals and tasks. Sometimes an inherited leadership in a family business may bring about organizational control by an individual indifferent to the task.

Some absentee leaderships are undertaken deliberately for protective reasons and provisions are made to avoid disrupting the organization. For example, a leading scientist in a highly specialized field may take the leadership of his professional institution to protect his particular field within it, and then delegate actual leadership roles to a second in command.

The extent to which the reasons for absentee leadership are conscious in the leader's mind, are part of public knowledge, derived from reasons that are on the table and acceptable to all concerned, with a compensating leadership functionally in place, the institution may function remarkably well. If a discrepancy exists between the formal table of organization and the actual workings of the organization's tasks, there is a risk of functional failure. Typical examples of such failure include a substitute leader who is overwhelmed by the organizational tasks, delegates them excessively to subordinates without clearly differentiating between strategic and tactical issues, overloads subordinates with problems that they cannot solve, and spends his own time with trivia rather than dealing with the central tasks of organizational leadership.

Or else, in the case of a narcissistic leader who goes through the motions, a ritualized fulfillment of organizational tasks may be expressed in chronic failure to fulfill commitments, evasive avoidance of decision making, and a consequent tendency to a growing isolation from each other of component task systems of the organization. As a consequence, the overall integration of institutional components gradually fails, irrational distribution of resources gradually develops, political struggle across task system boundaries erupts, and different departments and units get embroiled in chronic and often unnecessary contentiousness.

LEADERS WITH AFFECTIVE
UNAVAILABILITY OR INSTABILITY

So far, in describing leaders and the paranoiagenic effects of their failure, I have described leaders who present a relatively stable or normal capability of affective deployments. Sometimes leaders whose intelligence, moral integrity, conceptual clarity, and technical expertise all are excellent, may suffer from personality problems expressed particularly in the instability or unavailability of ordinary affective responses. These are usually, but not always, leaders who have significant pathology of internalized object relations.

Perhaps the most distinct type here is the "robot" leader, an individual who has enormous difficulty in expressing his own emotions and in accepting emotional expression in those who work with him. Persons with strongly obsessive or schizoid tendencies, and some narcissistic individuals may present these characteristics. Highly efficient in their communication around technical issues, they lack a dimension of humanity and therefore frustrate the emotional needs, particularly the dependency needs of those with whom they work, as well as exacerbating, by the absence of their emotional response, the paranoid tendencies among their subordinates. An organization's task systems may function effectively, but individuals in that institution may feel isolated, vaguely insecure, and with paranoid fears toward their inscrutable leadership.

The leader who is insecure in the realm of emotional expression may have the same effect as the absentee leader. If, however, he is strong in exercising decision-making and leadership functions in general, he may function well enough despite his "robot" characteristics. Unconsciously, leaders with these characteristics attempt to avoid intense emotional conflicts because of the threat of significant aggression evolving in these conflicts, and that fear communicates itself throughout the organization. This style of leadership discourages group processes within the organization, or rather fosters the development of what might be called an amorphous "crowd" of equally "self-controlled" "singletons," each having a sense of isolation and impotence, of not being able to influence the operations in the institution. Work may proceed satisfactorily, but typically is experienced as particularly exhausting because dependent needs of the staff are being frustrated.

In striking contrast to this absence of affective deployment, leaders with other significant personality disorders, particularly dependent, infantile, or histrionic, and borderline personalities tend to present intense emotional crises or temper tantrums as part of a leadership style that has significant disorganizing effects on their followers. Narcissistic, infantile, and dependent leaders may present themselves as overworked and exhausted and in dire need of soothing and support, which distracts their staff's attention from actual tasks, and transmits throughout the institution a general sense of "burnout."

"Burnout" symptoms—a general and persistent sense of exhaustion and of being overwhelmed—may also result from other leadership styles, particularly the narcissistic-charismatic leader who implicitly promises staff total gratification of all their needs, raises the level of expectation in unrealistic ways, and fails to set realistic limits to task performance. If the entire emotional life of the staff is to be gratified, in fantasy, at the workplace, "burnout" is a natural consequence. The emotional needs of the leader, and the staff's attention to the leader's needs, take precedence.

Temper tantrums of leaders with infantile or histrionic personality may, by direct expression of aggression in the context of organizational group processes, appear as a violent attack, an acute invasion of staff's privacy, what amounts to a traumatic group experience that may repeat itself frequently without the leader even being aware of having caused it. A dramatic decay of staff morale, high staff turnover, a chronic sense of frustration, failure, chaos, and terror may permeate the organization. The combination of such affective excesses with a paranoid leadership style may lead to a true "gaslight" atmosphere resulting in disastrous organizational disfunctioning.

It is rare for persons with such immature affective behavior to be promoted to the head of institutions, and, even though they possess unusual capacities in other areas, they tend to remain at an intermediate level of leadership; but because their emotional outbursts are directed largely against subordinates, it may take time before senior leadership becomes aware of them. However, an individual with strong narcissistic, paranoid, sadistic, and antisocial features (such as Hitler) may ascend to leadership as part of a "fight–flight" subgroup, and then stabilize such emotionally violent behavior in the context of a controlled, totalitarian bureaucracy, with maximal paranoiagenic effects.

A still different affective style that can be detrimental to organizational functioning is a certain superficial joviality that masks a deep emotional unavailability. Some narcissistic individuals adjust themselves only too well to the organizational hierarchical structure, ascend the hierarchical ladder by their remarkable flexibility, and end up in a position of authority where they apparently facilitate smooth functioning. But gradually a sense of unreality and emotional unavailability permeates the institution, needs for dependency are frustrated, and eventually the staff's sense of trust is undermined. Often such apparent friendliness and flexibility go hand in hand with a passive and conventional style of carrying out their task. Sudden crises exploding in their administrative realm may be the first indicator that something has been simmering under the surface for a long time.

THE CORRUPT LEADER

I am referring here to the leader who consciously and blatantly utilizes the organizational resources under his control for his own benefit, disregarding his responsibilities to the organization and to the task, and, in the process, clearly damages the organizational resources and task performance. The simple wish to maintain himself in power may be the dominant motivation for the leader's corrupt behavior, and this type of corruption is often to be found in a leader with a strong paranoid orientation and antisocial features, who visualizes the world as divided between friends and enemies, and for whom all measures at the service of survival are justified. Here is an example of the "paranoid urge to betray" described by Jacobson (1971); the paranoiagenic effects of this style of leadership stem more from the leader's paranoid behavior than from the corruption derived from it.

In contrast, corrupt behavior reflecting the leader's personal greed and voracity may present in individuals whose behavior is predominantly antisocial, and where paranoid tendencies emerge only when their exploitiveness and greed are threatened. Often narcissistic personalities with infantile tendencies and immature superego development perceive their leadership role as an entitlement as well as an opportunity for gratifying personal aspirations that would not otherwise be possible, an opportunity for accumulating wealth, gratification of particular sexual or dependent needs, and a willingness to reward those who collude with them in facilitating such accumulation. The complementary persecution and punishment of those who stand in the way of such exploitiveness or threaten him with public exposure create its paranoiagenic features.

A circle of corrupted followers friendly to the leader may create an entire layer of corrupt leadership. The group adopts the ideology that they constitute a leading class—for example, based on what they see as their historical rights, on their merits in ascending to leadership, or on the rationalization that they deserve compensation for their unusual, heavy responsibilities. The scandals about corrupt leadership in organizations whose goals are philanthropic or otherwise nonprofit in nature, and in political élites of long-standing social, or particularly, totalitarian regimes are examples.

It is usually a hierarchically rigid organization (such as a large bureaucracy) with enormous power invested at the top that permits the corrupt leader to develop a corrupt circle of influence around him, and the cascading paranoiagenic effects on the total organization may take time to develop. Usually, however, particularly in large organizations with multiple levels of hierarchy, implicit boundaries between the corrupt "inner circle" and the excluded "outer circle" tend to evolve, and, in the process, a sharp dividing line between the relaxed friendships on the top, and the resentment, suspicion, and paranoid fears of the excluded. One might consider this as the model case illustrating how psychopathic regression at one level generates a most powerful paranoid regression at the next level. The relationship between the Politbüro, on the one hand, and the lower levels of hierarchy of the Communist Party and the administrative structure of the German Democratic Republic, on the other, are illustrations (Schabowski, 1991). In small organizations, corrupt leadership may be replaced without major organizational turmoil; in large organizations, the widespread nature of institutional corruption means that a corrective organizational change will trigger intense paranoid regression throughout; the threat to organizational survival under such circumstances is maximal.

Narcissistic individuals with infantile and antisocial tendencies are the personalities who typically develop corrupt leadership. The temptations I have referred to in earlier work (Kernberg, 1991) explain why many corrupt leaders may have a history devoid of antisocial behavior before their rise to power, and their return to relatively normal social functioning after the collapse of their leadership role. It goes without saying that totalitarian regimes offer maximal possibilities and temptations for leadership corruption.

DIAGNOSIS AND MANAGEMENT

The task required to correct malfunctioning leadership is two-pronged: to diagnose the leader's functioning and the organizational dynamics and structure within which this functioning is taking place, and to manage the leader's malfunctioning and recognize what is required for restoring organizational health. The psychoanalytically oriented consultant has to be prepared to carry out this double function. Fortunately, for practical purposes, it is usually possible to integrate harmoniously organizational requirements and individual needs. A malfunctioning leader whose personality limitations are such that they do not permit him to carry out the corresponding organizational tasks, needs to be helped to shift his role, which, at the same time, also facilitates the reorganization of the organizational structure. Reorganization of institutional structures or tasks results in breaking the circular reaction of individual and group regression that causes the leader to function at his worst.

It should be kept in mind that the leader's personality problems are frequently the first symptom of organizational malfunctioning, and that it can happen that they are really no more than a symptom, that the cause of the organizational malfunctioning lies elsewhere. But when the leader's malfunctioning is indeed a significant factor in organizational malfunctioning, represented by the symptom of excessive paranoiagenesis, organizational and individual counseling reinforce each other.

It is important to separate organizational requirements from the leader's psychotherapeutic needs. The consultant diagnoses the institutional tasks not being accomplished; he explores whether the leader understands which tasks he did not accomplish and has the potential to do so, or whether it may require some time of testing to determine if he has the capacity to do so. Whether, in order to carry out these tasks, the leader will need personal treatment in addition to the consultative–educational process provided for him may have to be decided by the leader in the context of discussing the psychological issues involved in institutional management that are part of the consultative process.

Organizational consultation from a psychoanalytic viewpoint has to start at the top, with full authorization by the leadership of the organization, and then proceed through the exploration of organizational tasks, organizational structures, and of success and failure in organizational tasks under the condition of present or newly developing constraints. The study of group processes (by means of open group meetings in which work experiences are shared with the consultant within each level of hierarchical and task-system structure), jointly with interviews of key leaders in managerial positions, should permit carrying out an institutional diagnosis, and as part of it, a diagnosis of personality styles of leadership that are part of the problem.

Organizational counseling constitutes a second stage of the diagnostic enterprise; first of all, it is an institutional diagnosis that is required and that may lend itself to differentiate leaders' capacities to change their functioning once the nature of the difficulties that have been uncovered is clarified, and to diagnose the leader's limits to change. The organization should eventually be able to install and preserve a functional leadership and to carry out such changes as may be necessary to guarantee that.

An organizational consultation itself may temporarily increase paranoiagenesis in the institution; but fortunately, the liberating effect of an open ventilation of organizational conflicts that previously went underground or were expressed only through the rumor mill in itself tends to reduce paranoid developments. Much tension can be relieved by the consultative process, but there is also the risk of raising expectations of changes that may take time and be difficult to achieve. It is important, as part of organizational consultation, to discourage excessive idealization and messianic hopes, simultaneously with a focus on and resolution of the temporary accentuation of paranoiagenic regression.

If fundamental organizational changes are required that will affect the life of many individuals in the organization, the exploration of these changes may require first a confidential consultation with top leadership that may again temporarily increase paranoiagenesis. As soon as a point of closure has been achieved, however, there is an advantage in taking whatever corrective measures can be taken as quickly as possible, and to make them generally public as quickly as possible. When staff is fully informed of the facts, the reasons for change, and the nature of the change, paranoiagenesis tends to decrease remarkably even when the organization is in crisis.

I have been involved in two organizations in recent times which had to undergo a rapid reduction in staff, and, painful as the process was, it could be achieved without further organizational regression because once the impending changes were announced, the need for this significant reduction in the organization's workforce was universally recognized. The capacity of individuals and groups to trust their leaders when they are open and responsible is as great as their capacity for severe paranoid regression under conditions of organizational uncertainty and lack of open communication of unresolved problems.

REFERENCES

Bion, W. R. (1961), *Experiences in Groups*. New York: Basic Books.

Freud, S. (1921), Group psychology and the analysis of the ego. *Standard Edition*, 18:65–143. London: Hogarth Press, 1955.

Jacobson, E. (1971), Acting out and the urge to betray in paranoid patients. In: *Depression*. New York: International Universities Press, pp. 302–318.

Jaques, E. (1976), *A General Theory of Bureaucracy*. New York: Halsted.

Kernberg, O. F. (1979), Regression in organizational leadership. *Psychiatry*, 42:24–39.

———— (1991), The moral dimension of leadership. In: *Psychoanalytic Group Theory and Therapy: Essays in Honor of Saul Scheidlinger*, ed. S. Tuttman. Madison, CT: International Universities Press, pp. 87–112.

———— (1993), Paranoiagenesis in organizations. In: *Comprehensive Textbook of Group Psychotherapy*, 3rd ed., ed. H. Kaplan & B. J. Sadock. Baltimore: Williams & Wilkins, pp. 47–57.

Rice, A. K. (1965), *Learning for Leadership*. London: Tavistock Publications.

Schabowski, G. (1991), *Das Politbüro*. Reinbek bei Hamburg: Rowohlt Taschenbuch.

Turquet, P. (1975), Threats to identity in the large group. In: *The Large Group: Dynamics and Therapy*, ed. L. Kreeger. London: Constable, pp. 87–144.

6

Paranoid Symbol Formation in Social Organizations

Eric R. Marcus, M.D.

A medical student dormitory suffers an epidemic of gastroenteritis. The students become convinced that the food in their dining hall has been poisoned. They march en masse to the Dean of Students to protest. This case example is given to illustrate the type of paranoid process that social groups can organize. These paranoid phenomena are intense and frequent. There are many questions about their occurrence relating not only to paranoid processes in groups but also to the relationship between psychoanalysis and social science. For a psychoanalyst to "explain" paranoid social processes, some basic issues in social science must be joined.

Basic issues in social science have to do with phenomena of group behavior and cultural representations (Harris, 1968; Kuhns, 1983). Social science deals with the issue of similarities and differences between groups in behavior and cultural representations. In one school of cultural anthropology, adaptation to environment is an important variable related to cultural differences (Harris, 1968). My own psychoanalytic social science work follows this approach and looks at differences via adaptation.

The Columbia University Center for Psychoanalytic Training and Research has a long and productive history in this approach. It began with Kardiner. Kardiner worked with anthropologists at Columbia, among them Cora Du Bois, Ralph Linton, and Ruth Benedict (Manson, 1988). But he came to adaptation earlier in his career by working with the ego's adaptation to traumatic war experiences (Kardiner, 1941). Kardiner looked at adaptation as an independent and determining variable of group phenomena. He called the social organizations of this adaptation "primary institutions" to distinguish them from the "secondary institutions" which were dependent variables (Kardiner, 1939). Thus, myth was explained as a secondary institution related to the primary institution of child rearing as that process organized itself around family adaptation to the physical environment (Kardiner, 1939). Kardiner and Ovesey (1951), in a book on American blacks, their economic exploitation, and the result on their personality, continued this adaptational tradition. This tradition was also continued at Columbia Psychoanalytic by Hendin (1964) who explained differences in suicide rates and methods among the Scandinavian countries by describing the different psychological adaptations necessary to the different physical environments. He continued this work in his book *Black Suicide* (1969).

The exact mechanisms, however, relating adaption to intrapsychic phenomena and the structure of resulting representations, were left unclear. This was unfortunate because it left only the influence of the environment on child rearing as the causal pathway for entering adult individual psychology, and hence, adult group psychology. But there is a present and ongoing adaptational task. This may change dramatically during an adult's life; so may society. Social structure, in part, is organized in adaptation to this environment. Linkage points between this adaptational context and adult individual, hence, group psychology, are needed. How does the adaptational task enter the human psyche and what then happens? What is the definition of adaptation intrapsychically?

I have elsewhere likened adaptive task in reality to the day residue of a dream (Marcus, 1989). In looking at dreams medical students had about medical school, the adaptational task of their training appeared in the manifest content; for example, cutting the cadaver. This manifest content adaptational day residue was then symbolically altered by the primary process of the dream work. But does the adaptational task play a *specific* role in the primary process generation of an individual's specific symbolic structures? Can the same be said about cultural symbols or group behavior? If so, then the psychodynamics of these phenomena can perhaps be understood by looking at manifest content of group behavior and cultural representations as dream work in response to the adaptational day residue. One can see this by observing the adaptational task in reality and comparing it to the symbolic alterations of the adaptational task pictured in the manifest content. This method provides a linkage point between psychoanalysis and social science. Later, I will need another such linkage, a motivational one.

We can now look at similarities and differences in adaptation with a method for relating this independent variable to the dependent variable of social and cultural psychological phenomena.

This approach is quite different from the neoclassical Freudian approach in social science which looks at the content of cultural representations and describes them as derivatives of psychosexual stages with a view toward revealing universal themes regardless of differences between groups. The problem with this is its extension. Differences are then seen as merely an expression of the universal group fantasy without external causality. Roheim (1945) is an early example of this.

Followers of Klein, such as Bion (1959) and others, likewise describe universal group fantasies. They relate these fantasies to the vicissitudes of group process and to leadership, but without relating this to the adaptations required of natural social groups. But Bion did not work with such groups. He observed artificial, taskless, small groups. These highlight and exaggerate some group defenses but without a context as social science understands context. Michael Balint (1964) did look at psychological adaptation to social relationships in hospital and medical professional work groups. But he focused on adaptation as countertransference to medical patients' transference. For him, the adaptational task was a psychological one for both the independent and dependent variables; for both the adaptation context and the adaptation response.

When paranoid group enactments are considered, a psychoanalytic social science has immediate questions which must be addressed if the joint issues of content and structure of paranoid symptom formation and its adaptive function within group process are to be addressed. The first questions are: When and why do paranoid phenomena erupt in groups and social organizations? These questions must be addressed from the adaptational social science point of view and from the intra-psychic psychoanalytic point of view. The relationship must be exact and specific. A related problem is the aspect of defense. If such behavior is a defense, against what? Then there is the target of the paranoid behavior. Why is the specific target chosen and why in group process is the target often an aspect of reality?

I will, therefore, discuss the phenomenology of paranoid social processes with particular emphasis on the structure of their symbol formation whether in behavior or other cultural products. This will lead to a description of the affect and content. The affect and content will lead to a discussion of the defense problem and the target problem, which will lead to a discussion of the motivation problem.

In discussing these questions, I will try to keep clear the distinctions between individual psychology and group psychology; between individual psychic structure and the structure of group emotional responses; their enactments or representations. I am describing adaptationally evoked emotional representations and enactments. They may occur in individuals when they are part of certain groups. The total group response and its products has an intensity and a summated content that may be lacking in any one individual. Group psychology under this model becomes, therefore, the hypothesized construct of a group as a single individual.

We must be careful, however, in applying individual psychoanalytic psychology to groups, especially psychoanalytic metapsychology. The problems of definition, of semantics, and of relationship to observation, all are magnified if one directly applies metapsychology to groups. This is especially so if one considers a group a hypothetical person. A group does not have an inborn instinctual nature, nor a psychological structure except as it is a collection of individuals. However, groups do not act as merely a collection of individuals, but, rather, with certain responses that are only seen when the individuals form a group. In this sense, the group is like a new and unique single individual rather than a collection of individuals. But this does not mean that metapsychology of the individual can be automatically applied. "Group" and "individual" are different conceptualizations. I cannot in this paper deal with all these issues thoroughly. I will, therefore, try to stick close to observation and descriptive phenomenology.

THE STRUCTURE OF PARANOID SYMBOL
FORMATION IN SOCIAL ORGANIZATIONS

I shall continue with the story about the medical students' poisoning to provide an illustration of the structure of these phenomena. The structure of this particular example illustrates how such paranoid group eruptions often occur.

The medical students did run to the Dean of Students. They confronted the Dean with their conviction that they were being poisoned. The Dean of Students, a direct, forceful, action-oriented person, sent the students over to the student health service for culture of their diarrhea and vomitus. The food in the dormitory was also cultured. This calmed the students down—something was being done. They were being taken seriously. A week later the results of the laboratory tests were back—viral gastroenteritis! The remnants of the paranoid process evaporated.

To understand what happened, both paranoid eruption and "cure," you need to know the adaptational context of medical student life in reality. The students had been agitating for more free time in their impacted curriculum. At a series of early morning meetings with the faculty, some free time was carved out; one afternoon a week. Unbeknownst to the students, the faculty then inserted another course into that time. Although it was a course that the students had also been agitating for, they had not planned to give up the free time they had so laboriously won. No announcement of this fact took place. The students discovered it when they read the newly published schedule of their classes. The faculty, as can be guessed from the story, was never in favor of the free time.

In this reality context, it is more intuitively understandable that: (1) the students had feelings of anger and betrayal; (2) the idea that something really did happen; (3) their choice of the Dean of Students as target of the solution (a person whom the students believed had authority and power to be used for their benefit); and (4) their displacement of affect to the targets of the projection, the food, the food handlers, and the Dean of Students. The projection target was multiple although related. The exact target was unclear. Was it the food, the food handlers, the Dean of Students, the medical school at large, or all of these? It is interesting to note that the reality day residue was likewise difficult to locate. Was it individual faculty, the curriculum committee, the entire medical school faculty, or all of these? The conceptual day residue and the conceptual displaced target of the projection, however, were the medical school in its caretaking function.

The betrayal dynamics seem to be something like this. The students awoke one day to find they felt as if they had been poisoned. And they had been: their curriculum, their time, their trust, their autonomy, and their hopes for power were all poisoned. This left them in a humiliating, running, emotional rage like diarrhea, feeling they were treated like shit; their voluminous, curricular aspirations flushed away.

Now, I believe the structure of paranoid symptoms in social groups and organizations may have a predictable form. The phenomena, whether behavioral or cultural product, starts as a reality day residue. This day residue involves the limitations on task inherent in inadequate resources; in the students' case, it was time. Sometimes these resources are perceived by the unconscious, and in reality actually are unequally distributed. Often, an abrupt change in the allocation of resources has occurred. Resources have been reallocated or "grabbed." The knowledge of this grabbing of resources may be conscious or unconscious but it is often dissociated from the ensuing paranoid phenomena. The rage and betrayal evoked by the event are then focused on a target. The target is an object in reality that bears an associational relevance to the day residue. Often, the target object in reality is a displaced aspect or aspects of the causal feature in the original day residue. The displacement occurs "because" access to the causal day residue is blocked; either the causal day residue is hidden or diffuse, or guarded by powerful retaliatory forces within the organization. The projection of the group is onto an aspect of the social environment which symbolically represents, according to the primary process, the function of society that has been betrayed by the reality day residue. In the medical student case, it was the caretaking function of the medical school in its charge to intellectually nurture and feed the medical students in a responsible way. The reality day residue evokes task specific emotional reactions that are further shaped and organized by task specific defenses, and by the social system adaptation, which is itself partly organized by these task specific group defenses. The result of these day residue events and dynamic primary process responses in paranoid group reactions is a primary process projection of malevolence, rage, and betrayal. In fact, the paranoid group often has been betrayed, but from indifference, callousness, and greed not necessarily malevolence and rage.

Sometimes, the displaced target is a disadvantaged victim subgroup used in a paranoid way as a scapegoat. This subgroup is often a demander or user of scarce resources but not the major one, which is either hidden or guarded. The medical students and their time demands on the faculty is an example. Medical student teaching takes an enormous amount of time from faculty which is not well rewarded in the faculty promotional system. But the main faculty drain is research grantsmanship which requires one quarter of faculty time, vastly greater than anyone's teaching commitment but about which the faculty can do nothing. Every moment spent teaching is a moment away from grant seeking. At the same time, faculty departments act as if the curriculum is their turf, and for some, it does provide the only reason for surviving as a separate department.

The summary of paranoid dynamics in social groups and organizations, therefore, is that when there is a severe task constraint that is unequally distributed in the organization and when this unequal distribution is hidden or protected, then there will be high likelihood of an acute or chronic paranoid reaction. What this means is that when one observes a paranoid group one can suspect an unequal, unfair, and hidden distribution of technological, financial, or time resources. I am talking about alterations in the relationship of needed resources to required task. For instance, it takes students a certain amount of time to learn.

To what extent do privileged social groups with narcissistic dynamics defending against guilt have paranoid reactions to attempts against a just redistribution of resources? Psychoanalytic social science research is needed to answer this important question.

The hidden nature of the day residue evoker or the abruptness of its revelation, or the constraints on direct attack against the offending group, which is often more powerful, any or all of these results in an intense primary process eruption. This is because the evoked affect is intense and also because discharge along reality mastery channels is blocked by the social system. This is especially intense if survival seems threatened. Then, the intense emotional reaction erupts into consciousness and captures, through primary process condensation, the original day residue, or, usually a displaced day residue or day residue aspect. *This merging of a displaced day residue of survival importance with a primary process rage eruption forms the structure of these paranoid symbolic alterations of reality that make up the structure of paranoid group representations and enactments.*

Like higher borderline states, the day residue of paranoid phenomena may be conscious but dissociated and displaced or, like lower borderline states, preconscious and condensed along with the symbolic alteration of reality that has occurred (Marcus, 1992, p. 51). The affect evoked by the day residue is not only experienced but projected in the condensed symbolic alteration of reality onto a new, displaced real object. This affect response is the leading edge of the psychological processes that are mobilized in an attempt to adapt to the betrayal inherent in the actual day residue.

AFFECT

The affect evoked by the paranoid symbol's day residue is rage and betrayal. It is an intense aggression that has elements of fear and desperation. The fear and desperation are warded off to varying degrees but never completely. The desperation has to do with the betrayed dependency state. Students are dependent on faculty for knowledge, organization of learning, and certification through grades and graduation. Their fear is due to the conflict between their rage and their dependency. The dependency yearning, to be well taken care of, is part of the attachment need. The dependency yearning and desperate rage-fear give the paranoid group attachment affect its particular quality. This fear and rage, when intense, infiltrate all levels and aspects of these affect dynamics, their representations, and enactments. It is the affect sine qua non of paranoid groups.

If the projection eases, real injustice to the original day residue is clear and is better contained in secondary process. The injustice of the projection is then also much clearer. In this case, the hidden food handlers were bearing the brunt. Guilt then may become apparent. The guilt is usually handled by resolving paranoid groups through various forms of denial; of fact, of significance, of degree, rather than through atonement and reparation. This is because the group guilt is expiated by the real betrayal deprivation the group suffered.

The point is that survival aggression seems much more powerful an affect driving force of paranoid phenomena in social institutions than libido. Adaptation to insure survival seems to mobilize intense aggression both in the service of mastery and in the service of destructive power attempting to smash constraint. This is a part of the desperate adaptation tactics of survival. To the extent that libido is mobilized, it is often the oral fantasies of dependency rage that social process attempts to organize as a crucial aspect of its raison d'etre. To the extent that attachment is a necessity for survival, to the extent that this necessitates a relationship to a cruel, betraying social object, to this extent will the evoked, condensed, paranoid, aggressive, and secondary libidinal fantasies be organized around oral sadomasochistic themes.

DEFENSES

The concept of defense applies to individual psychology. Can it also apply to group psychology and, if so, to what extent? I believe the concept can apply to a limited extent to group phenomena. Groups do show emotional reactions which unfold over time in certain contexts. One can make certain interventions which influence those evolving unfoldings and then see shifts and reorganizations, as when the Dean sent the students for medical tests. In this sense, the concept of defense seems to hold. In addition, one can see varying organizations of those defenses analogous to neurotic, borderline, or psychotic levels, depending on relationships to day residue, relationship to primary processing, and level of reality testing.

Defenses in paranoid group eruptions are complex. They defend against the reality day residue which if recognized fully, might lead to behavior dangerous to the subgroup because of the other, betraying group's power. The defenses must also defend against the affects of rage, fear, guilt, and dependency. Often, the condensation fantasy that best organizes these themes is the paranoid sadomasochistic fantasy.

These sadomasochistic paranoid themes involve condensations of aggression, libido, defenses against aggression projected as sadism in the object, and guilt against aggression organized as masochistic group self-experience which is then further evocative of aggressive defenses, and, thus, warded off in Bion's fight or flight (Bion, 1959).

Masochistic organizations of paranoid group fantasies are common. It is one aspect of the pressure to scapegoat. The need is to reverse the masochistic position with its affects of shame, humiliation, and failure to thrive. This gets intensified when the masochistic group finds its survival threatened. Particularly when a subgroup is under almost total domination, will sadomasochistic organization emerge.

Again, medical student culture is full of examples. Here is an example of a typical cadaver dream from medical school:

> I dreamt that I was in a cemetery at night and all the bodies which were buried in the ground covered with a cloth weren't "in" the ground. The bodies were in two rows lined up. I was looking for a particular body. I walked from body to body lifting up the covers. Suddenly, some of the corpses starting waking up as I disturbed them. Lifting their heads, they started standing up and were angry that I was there in their domain. They suddenly all stood up and chased me. I ran outside the gate of the cemetery. I just kept going. I knew they were close on my heels.

The defense against the deprivation resulting from the real social betrayal must defend against two aspects of the deprivation situation. One is the external reality of the betrayal-deprivation. This must be defended against because of the fear that action for mastery will break the social bond between subgroups and the betrayed will end up with even less or will be attacked. The other is the internal, psychological rage—survival anxiety. When betrayal-deprivation is involved, rage and survival fear are evoked. This is defended against by projection lest it cause the subgroup to break the bond. In typical borderline fashion, the group not only projects the malevolence but also feels the malevolence in itself, but only, it feels, in response (Marcus, 1992, chapter 3). But the group's rage is threatening to itself not mainly because of guilt but because of fears of loss-abandonment. A dependent social subgroup, like children, fears abandonment threats to survival even more than malevolence. The same is true in complex societies which involve complex socioeconomic interdependencies that are profound survival mediators.

This discussion of affect and of defenses leads to a conclusion about the resulting dynamics. It is the dynamics of aggression with evoked, reparative libido. This leads to a further need for elaboration of the theory of aggression, in this case, survival aggression. This may be linked to theories of ego mastery. It requires another linkage point between psychoanalysis and social science. The link is through the ego; through reality. This requires that psychoanalysis deal with the issues of survival and mastery inherent in social adaptation whether within a culture or a social organization or an individual. Where is survival in Freudian motivational theory?

EGO INSTINCTS

As extensively discussed in Laplanche and Pontalis (1973), Freud wrestled with this issue early in his career when he discussed the ego instincts which were one of the forces opposing libido and the first that he proposed. Although he dropped this view early on, he never repudiated the view that the ego has its own survival motivation and drive energy, although he was using ego to mean self in those early days before the structural theory. Hartmann (1958) elaborated on the issue as part of the structural theory, where ego meant reality mediating functions of human mental experience. The intensity, tenacity, and organizing power of this aspect of human motivation has been underestimated by neoclassical psychoanalysts. In social science, it has resulted in focusing on universal aspects of sexual fantasy, in status nascendi.

If we go back to Freud's 1905 "Three Essays on the Theory of Sexuality," we find him saying that the sexual instincts first come into existence by "attaching themselves" to survival needs (Laplanche and Pontalis, 1973). Only later do the sexual instincts take their own path, but never completely so. Because social groups exist in part, I think, as an adaptational strategy for self-survival, such groups recapitulate early oral dependency anxieties and wishes. These oral anxieties power the regressions so ubiquitous and so dramatic in these groups.

The advantage to reconsidering the concept of survival instincts, or ego instincts, linked to aggression and linked to but separate from oral libido is the explanatory power derived from having a heuristic concept which coincides with various observations. The psychopathology of groups involves intense aggression. The defenses against the aggression attempt not only to smash but to maintain the intergroup bond. The primitive projection responses and sadomasochistic defenses seem to involve issues of competitive adaptation. The day residue observed seems closely linked to competitive adaptation and to survival constraint. The behavior in reality of social groups, the day residue of these fantasies, and their representations and enactments, all seem to involve these issues.

In groups or even in individuals, the issue of separate drive states versus one condensed drive state can, at this time in scientific progress, be only a semantic or heuristic argument. But heuristically it is helpful to consider that aggression can have some autonomy at least in its intensity. This is heuristically helpful because one observes the condensed libido aggression fantasy change as the intensity of the frustration rage increases. This is true of all primary process/drive relationships. In groups, the same is observationally true for survival anxiety.

This view of motivation, thus, seems more parsimoniously and directly related to the observations of group phenomena, and also is more directly applicable to social science observations and concerns. It is a second crucial link point. The libido motivational link point between neoclassical psychoanalysis and social science has difficulties in application unless one takes the step of situation evoked libido. I do take this step; so did Freud. Quoted in Wortis' book about his analysis with Freud, he has Freud saying that if one wished to talk about competitive aggression elicited by some types of societies, "that would be worth talking about" (Wortis, 1950, p. 130; see also p. 60).

The fact remains that aggression is the overwhelming affect in these phenomena and this coincides more with Freud's later dual instinct theories. But desdrudo is an aggression/death instinct, not an aggression/survival instinct (Laplanche and Pontalis, 1973) and so we are returned to the original ego instincts of survival, which offers us the best heuristic possibility for a more complete psychoanalytic social science.

Explication of these observations about group aggression and survival as applicable to individuals, their psychology and metapsychology is an interesting topic that goes beyond the scope of this paper. But Freud did understand this issue. He talked about mastery instinct and motivation. He was also, of course, aware of the problem of unitary versus separate drives and the problem of mastery strivings in this regard. Freud (1905):

> At about the same time as the sexual life of children reaches its first peak, between the ages of three and five, they also begin to show signs of the activity which may be ascribed to the instinct for knowledge or research. This instinct cannot be counted among the elementary instinctual components, nor can it be classed as exclusively belonging to sexuality [p. 194].

Mastery is an inborn aspect of maturation that influences development in all structural spheres including motivation, and may become involved in psychic conflict. Freud came to think of this as true for all instincts (Laplanche and Pontalis, 1973). I suspect this is true for survival as well.

REFERENCES

Balint, M. (1964), *The Doctor, His Patient, and the Illness*. New York: International Universities Press.

Bion, W. R. (1959), *Experiences in Groups*. London: Tavistock.

Freud, S. (1905), Three Essays on the Theory of Sexuality. *Standard Edition*, 7:125–243. London: Hogarth Press, 1953.

Harris, M. (1968), *The Rise of Anthropological Theory*. New York: T. Y. Crowell.

Hartmann, H. (1958), *Ego Psychology and the Problem of Adaptation*. New York: International Universities Press.

Hendin, H. (1964), *Suicide and Scandinavia*. New York: Grune & Stratton.

———— (1969), *Black Suicide*. New York: Basic Books.

Kardiner, A. (1939), *The Individual and His Society*. New York: Columbia University Press.

———— (1941), *The Traumatic Neuroses of War*. Washington, DC: National Research Council.

———— Ovesey, L. (1951), *The Mark of Oppression*. Cleveland: Meridian, 1969.

Kuhns, R. (1983), *Psychoanalytic Theory of Art*. New York: Columbia University Press.

Laplanche, J., & Pontalis, J.-B. (1973), *The Language of Psychoanalysis*. New York: W. W. Norton.

Manson, W. (1988), *The Psychodynamics of Culture*. New York: Greenwood Press.

Marcus, E. R. (1989), Psychoanalysis and social science research; Medical student dreams about medical school. Paper presented to the American Psychoanalytic Association, December.

———— (1992), *Psychosis and Near Psychosis: Ego Function, Symbol Structure, Treatment*. New York: Springer-Verlag.

Roheim, G. (1945), *The Eternal Ones of the Dream*. New York: International Universities Press.

Wortis, J. (1950), *Fragments of an Analysis with Freud*. New York: McGraw-Hill, 1975.

Part III

Paranoia in Clinical Work

7

Paranoid Betrayal and Jealousy: The Loss and Restitution of Object Constancy

Harold P. Blum, M.D.

Paranoia, in all its individual, group, and social manifestations, remains a most important area for further clinical investigation and theoretical conceptualization. More than any other psychopathology, it is associated with danger to the individual and to his or her object relations. On a social scale, especially in the age of modern weapons, it threatens the imposition and maintenance of omnipotent tyranny, the provocation of wars with the potential for limitless destruction and suffering in which the very survival of humanity may be threatened. Full-blown cases of paranoia are not individually analyzable and often do not seek treatment because of distrust and suspicion, hatred, and fear of persecutory victimization. Paranoid tendencies can be analyzed, but rarely the fixed paranoid personality. Applications of psychoanalysis, not only to case histories such as Schreber (Freud, 1911), but also to psychotherapy and opportunities for analytic observation and inferences are of crucial importance.

Anyone may, under particular circumstances, develop paranoid regression, usually in transient form. The paranoia may be circumscribed or encapsulated, limited or pervasive, or may be mainly within a group process or special social structure. There are paranoid states, groups, and leaderships, and a range of individuals from those with mild paranoid tendencies to the paranoid personality to paranoid psychosis. We are all familiar with the tendency to idealize the group with whom one identifies, to distrust and project all evil and hostility to others outside the group. This leads to an idealized in-group and a devalued and often threatening out-group, with good and bad objects and collective objects. Psychoanalysis is not unacquainted with such groups in its own history, and the tendencies toward splitting, idealization, and devaluation have also been responsible, at times, for the splitting of societies and institutes. Paranoid processes (Meissner, 1978) may be discerned in attachment to various sects, causes, and ideologies. Paranoid sects devalue and persecute those who are seen as opposed to their narcissistically invested belief system or as adherents of alternate systems and different beliefs. Individual deviation may be scapegoated or persecuted as heresy.

Paranoid attitudes and ideation are potentially universal responses, although individual proclivities show tremendous variations. Those individuals with paranoid proclivities are more readily attracted and susceptible to paranoid group attitudes and readily seek paranoid leaders. On the other hand, some individuals, fearful of domination and persecutory abuse, may struggle against or rebel at any sign of tyrannical domination. They may be vigilant guardians of civil liberty. A little paranoia may go a long way toward recognition of the abuse and corruption of power.

Methodologically, it is important to keep in mind that the earliest theories of paranoia were based upon applied analysis with minimal clinical contact with paranoid patients. The psychopathology may be considerably varied in different cases, but certain common features have been found.

This paper will deal with paranoid personality and a particular clinical example of paranoid jealousy and betrayal to illustrate, elucidate, and expand recent work on the subject (Blum, 1980, 1981). In addition to the role of malignant narcissism (Kernberg, 1975), hatred, aggression, projection, and splitting of the ego, I shall emphasize the failure to negotiate separation-individuation and the regressive loss of object constancy. This is associated with a desperate effort to reestablish a relationship with the inconstant object. The inconstant object is the negative of libidinal object constancy, the hostile selfobject or persecutory narcissistic object to which an attachment is sought and maintained or reestablished at all costs. Attachment after detachment becomes a desperate tie for survival; even if this relationship is regarded as dangerous, it is the lesser evil when compared to objectless disorganization. This is a contemporary revision of Freud's proposition of the delusional reconstruction of the lost object world. The narcissistic system of megalomania and persecutory object relationship attempts to preserve the crucial relationship with the inconstant narcissistic object. Extreme love/hate ambivalence with predominant projection of murderous hatred and self-hatred prevails. Separation-individuation has not been successfully negotiated, and narcissistic and structural regression occur coincident with the onset of parnaoia. Attacks by or on the self or object, fears of loss, invasion, or merger are readily fused and confused because of incomplete selfobject differentiation and lack of stable intrapsychic representation. The concern with boundaries and betrayal, allies and enemies is reflected in the institutionalized paranoia of totalitarian tyranny. The nation's boundaries must be defended with armor, and engulfment of other territory coexists with fear of destructive invasion and engulfment.

In the paranoid personality there are many areas of intact object relations, identity, and ego functioning, but within the paranoid there is always some regressive loss of object constancy associated with impaired reality-testing and reliance upon the predominant defense of projection. The rather exclusive reliance on projection may be constitutionally determined and is, in turn, associated with a compromise of reality testing; but the reality testing function in itself may be constitutionally fragile or impaired by conflict and trauma.

There are three other features of the paranoid personality that I wish to emphasize, and all are related to the issue of the historical truth in the delusion (Freud, 1937). The first of these features is the probability of the history of an infantile or childhood paranoid tendency, exemplified in the history of the Wolf Man (Freud, 1918; Blum, 1974). In my experience, close examination of these patients will often show pronounced narcissistic and masochistic features already discernible in childhood. There may have been "lifelong" paranoid tendencies toward suspicion, mistrust, and susceptibility to feelings of injury and insult. Feelings of being watched, scrutinized, and criticized are common, with superego regression and externalization. In childhood, these patients are often narcissistically withdrawn loners, given to excessive, self-absorbed, sadomasochistic, self-glorifying day-dreaming, and solitary play. Others have displayed a veneer of friendliness or disarming seduction. Nightmares are often recalled in which the patient is the object of terrorized attack and helplessness in the face of assault and infantile tantrums of screaming, raging, attack, and fearing attack may not be atypical. Nightmares often repeat and represent traumatic situations and are not pathognomonic of any specific disorder. But nightmares in these patients may leave a "hangover effect," and as in children are, at first, poorly differentiated from reality. The "paranoid" nightmare invades reality.

One such adult paranoid patient was noted to have attempted to assault his newborn sibling and pummeled his mother's abdomen and thighs in an impotent rage. He screamed words of abuse at his mother and later felt that she wanted to evict him from the household as he had earlier wanted to eliminate his new sibling rival. He was studious in school but could not sustain friendships, and became an ungainly, unpopular adolescent. Then he became frankly paranoid in young adulthood. He was convinced that his peers were hostile because of his superior talents and was suspicious that his parents might conspire against him with peers whose friendship he had avoided or alienated. His peers represented his despised sibling and his self-hate.

The second point, also related to historical truth, is the actuality of psychological abuse or traumatic experience (Frosch, 1990), which serves as narcissistic injury, eliciting aggression. Every traumatic experience, overwhelming in nature, inevitably involves narcissistic mortification and the terror of helplessness. Also, many of these patients have been narcissistically traumatized, deeply hurt, and humiliated. Identifications with paranoid parents are not infrequent, and some paranoid dispositions are anchored in familial styles of scapegoating, blaming, and victimization.

The truth in the delusion (Freud, 1937) also rests in the paranoid individual's supersensitive perception of the jealousy and hostility of others. What are correctly recognized as the malevolent wishes of others may be exaggerated in importance, while the same impulses are denied, projected, and minimized in the self. However, the paranoid's own suspiciousness and hostility may be noted by others, arousing their fear and aggression and anchoring the suspiciousness of the paranoid personality in current reality. Freud (1922) noted the presence of impulses toward infidelity in both partners, and the tendency of the paranoid personality to recognize and exaggerate the imagined infidelity of the partner. Envy, jealousy, and betrayal are denied and projected onto the partner, and the paranoid tends to cling to the position of innocent victim. Responsibility for injury or misfortune is evaded. Since blame and guilt are projected, the paranoid is indignant, self-righteous, and litigious, demanding and redressing injury. The collection of injustice and wrongs that must but cannot be righted, reinforces the urge toward betrayal as a means of vindication, vengeance, and mastery. The urge to betray avoids passivity and is also a preemptive strike against the disloyal inconstant object.

The paranoid personality retreats to previous narcissistic fixations, reactivating and reinforcing previous narcissistic injuries, and lacks the resilience to overcome such narcissistic hurts. Deep-seated feelings of inadequacy and inferiority coexist with grandiosity. The paranoid individual is vindictive and vengeful, carrying a willful ill-will or grudge that seems to have a life of its own. Paranoid vengefulness is unforgiving and tends to be ruthless and remorseless (Socarides, 1966). Omnipotent and compensatory narcissistic aggrandizement and narcissistic rage are directed against undoing and reversing traumatic helplessness and avenging the previous narcissistic injury (Kohut, 1972). Passivity is evaded and denied, and the paranoid personality scans, plans, plots, and always remains vigilant for possible victimization. Markedly exaggerated responses to the slightest slight or social injury were noted by Freud (1911), associated with reactivation of traumatic narcissistic disappointments and injuries of preadult life. While the persecutory system shows features from all levels of development, the threats to narcissistic equilibrium, the fragility of self-esteem, and the readiness to utilize projection and denial are most characteristic of early childhood. This is consonant with infantile pathogenic determinants, and there has been a shift in the understanding of paranoia in three different directions.

The first is a shift away from emphasis upon the negative Oedipus complex and repressed homosexuality, emphasized by Freud in the midperiod of his thinking on paranoia, between 1910 and 1920. Murderous hostility is far more important than homosexual love. The second is a view of pathogenesis which stresses preoedipal roots and determinants. The third is a recognition of the relative importance of later phases of development, particular insofar as they may fortify earlier paranoid tendencies or allow for later beneficial reorganization and developmental mastery. While adult paranoid tendencies have important genetic antecedents and infantile prototypes, not all children with paranoid tendencies develop paranoia as adults. Nor is adult paranoia usually reducible to a single, simple infantile template or prototype, a genetic fallacy.

I shall now turn to a case of Dr. Jekyll and Mr. Hyde. In Dr. H paranoid jealousy and vindictiveness were associated with fears of and urges toward betrayal and persecution. The underlying narcissistic rage and murderous feelings, almost without conscious guilt and with extremely guarded attitudes, made extraordinary demands even on the supervision of his treatment. Dr. H started treatment because of a marital crisis, rampant infidelity, and fears of his wife's infidelity. A medical resident, he was afraid he didn't get along with people, in general, especially his wife. He could easily get into arguments with fellow house staff as well as patients. At the time he started treatment, he had two small children. His arguments with his wife concerned mutual accusations of infidelity, his not helping her with child rearing, and her own needs for intimacy and companionship. She wasn't nearly as sexually gratifying as the women of his affairs, nurses and patients. About to complete the transition from fellowship to private work, he had a perfectionistic attitude. He was particularly concerned about his difficulties in patient care, worried that he might make a mistake in diagnosis or treatment. He was a serious student of medicine, consistently trying to master more of the subject, protecting and defending against competitive feelings toward other doctors.

The fights with his wife took the form of shouting and screaming arguments, with his own threats of desertion and his wife's threats of divorce. He had become so contemptuous of his wife that he no longer tried to be particularly discreet about his affairs. At one time, his wife caught him and informed the woman's husband. He dismissed fears of the husband's rage, but quickly betrayed and exchanged this partner for another, a repetitive pattern. He was far more fearful of being caught moonlighting or occasionally stealing petty items for personal or family use from the "stingy" hospital.

He thought that his suspicion and anger about his wife might have begun at the time she had a postpartum depression following the birth of their second child. He knew he was annoyed at her for not being available to him or the children, the very complaints that she had about him. While his tendencies toward promiscuity preexisted her depression, they probably were exacerbated. He would lie to his wife without real feelings of remorse, and he promised fidelity when he was caught. However, any notion of reciprocal infidelity on her part would be considered a massive betrayal and outrageous disloyalty, and he was increasingly suspicious. He apparently had a masked postpartum paranoia concurrent with his wife's postpartum depression.

The immediate conscious precipitant for his coming for help was his wife's threatening divorce and demanding he get help as a possible condition for maintaining the marriage. Separation is always a threat in paranoia, but separateness and intrapsychic narcissistic object relationship were crucial. He felt betrayed when she was emotionally unavailable due to her maternity and her depression. He took his wife's threats more seriously because he suspected she had a partner waiting in the wings, and, therefore, she found divorce to be tolerable. He rationalized his affairs since various hypochondriacal symptoms such as chest pain and headaches disappeared during the time he was having an affair. The affairs were comforting and soothing and represented (from his point of view) revenge against his insensitive and depriving wife. Furthermore, if he was not having an affair, he began to have frightening rape fantasies. These sadomasochistic fantasies involved awesome power of domination and humiliation over his female victim. He was the omnipotent aggressor, not the traumatized victim. His fantasy victim had to beg for her life. He was a Don Juan who sought ever-new conquests but who could not allow himself to depend upon any one woman. He was forever in search of an ideal giving woman but always felt disappointed, teased, frustrated, and finally angry enough to coerce and compel gratification. Behind a thin veneer of complacency and a facade of friendliness, he was "walking wounded," chronically dissatisfied, hurt and angry, and a predator ready to pounce on available prey.

He also recognized that he was psychologically divorced from his wife even before she could divorce him. Along with his rage at her for her fantasied betrayals, there was also a feeling of good riddance toward her and toward all his previous women. His need for attachment and detachment preserved the object tie and defended against object dependency and engulfment. As time went on he had become more self-absorbed and more angry. Each disappointment in "love" led to bilateral feelings of rejection, accumulated resentment, and urges for new attachment. He suspected that his wife was now going to betray him and that he would take an emotional and financial beating in the divorce. Marriage was a terrible trap, but divorce was a terrifying loss.

During his period of treatment, the therapist was regarded as a possible friend-in-need; the treatment had a modicum of hope, and the distrust, suspicion, and antagonism were largely focused upon his wife. He was, of course, also suspicious and guarded in the treatment. He was concerned about anonymity and confidentiality and whether the therapist was truly motivated to help him. What were the therapist's ulterior motives, and did he desire to dominate and control the patient, and would he be victimized? Would the male therapist be interested in dating the patient's wife if she were to divorce the patient? Would he testify in court if the patient were involved in a divorce, and were his secrets safe? The paranoid patient's concern with secrets is overdetermined; for example, by shame and threats of self-esteem. But at bottom, it is related to the preservation of boundaries and to magical control of and by the narcissistic object.

There were certainly elements of positive transference, some small capacity for an alliance of help and protection against victimization. He needed an ally against his enemies. The therapist and therapy might help him regain his confidence and sense of security and stability; but his ally could betray and change from friend to foe, Jekyll to Hyde. He was fearful of acting on his rage fantasies and aware of a rising threat of violence, both toward and within him. The reliability and predictability of the therapeutic situation and the accepting tolerant attitude of the therapist were real factors which helped to create a calm, tolerant therapeutic holding environment for this patient. Nevertheless, he was constantly screening the situation to determine whether the therapist was friend or foe. He was suspicious and guarded, but involved and forthright. He retained some hope that therapy would help, but he was more concerned with testing the safety of the situation so that he would not be victimized. Therapy proceeded against this background of limited faith, fear of betrayal, and constant testing of the therapist's therapeutic commitment, candor, and capacity to tolerate and contain his aggression. The therapist was also sought as a benign, external superego who would help him with self-esteem regulation and impulse control. With patients like this countertransference reactions may be intense, and the therapist may become preoccupied and hypervigilant and paranoid toward and about the patient.

I shall now briefly summarize the salient history which emerged, piecemeal, during the almost three years of psychotherapy. The patient was the oldest child of nonreligious Protestant parents from a medium-sized, Mid-West community. He had no memories before 3 to 4 years of age, but had been repeatedly told about his mother's postpartum depression continuing after his birth. But there were much more immediate memories associated with feeling frightened, alone, and at peril which he now thought the therapist ought to know.

He was always anxious, and this had been heightened during medical school. His anxiety, however, reached a fever-pitch during brief reserve military service. He had received a phone call threatening him with death, and he had sat awake all night long with a gun at his side. He then became afraid of dying in an accident which was, in turn, followed by concerns about death in the surrounding population. He developed ideas that the food was poisoned and became extremely careful about the foods he allowed himself to eat. Had he been ready for the "funny farm," he wondered. He thought he was having delusions, but at the same time believed he was really in danger and could be poisoned to death. He remained perplexed by the appearance and disappearance of this transient paranoid psychosis.

His recall of this episode proved to be related to a most remarkable current complementary circumstance. The patient, it turned out, had written inappropriate medication orders for his own patients—orders in which the wrong dose of a drug or an inappropriate drug were prescribed. These orders had been arranged to be observed by other members of the medical staff and were countermanded. Dr. H, who was afraid of being poisoned, was in danger of poisoning his own patients. The fear of persecution and retaliation had masked the wish to persecute. He was now frightened that murderous fantasies could be a reality. He seemed struck by some capacity for concern and guilt, although the therapist was also aware of a malicious indifference or even pleasure at the idea of injuring his own patients. Medicine had always had multiple appeals: he could heal himself and his mother; it offered the power of life and death, of inflicting and undoing injury and trauma; and also it was an opportunity to satisfy his voyeurism and his predatory sexual and aggressive impulses. His paranoia was largely outside the transference, so that the therapist was "Dr. Jekyll," and his own treatment was preserved.

The threat of independent management and mismanagement and the unconscious fantasy of maiming or murder of his own patients, was a major underlying issue in treatment. Responsibility for medical management could threaten destabilization and regression. What poisoned the atmosphere at home and in the hospital was not a homosexual panic, so much as the threat of murder and being murdered. In turn, his murderous rage was interwoven with and displaced from the particular target of his inconstant wife whom he felt had betrayed him. This violently jealous, possessive patient could not live with his wife, but he also could not live without her. She represented a primary object, a beacon of orientation (Mahler, 1971), an auxiliary ego (A. Freud, 1965), and the narcissistic object with whom he sought to maintain or reestablish object constancy (McDevitt, 1975). He defensively retreated from oedipal and homosexual conflicts, but his oedipal organization was a superstructure based upon a fragile preoedipal, narcissistic foundation.

The patient had consulted a general psychiatrist before starting treatment that was a combination of expressive and supportive analytic psychotherapy. Sent for psychological tests which indicated the possibility of psychosis, the patient had wondered if the doctor were trying to tell him that he was an incurable paranoid schizophrenic. He was placed on tranquilizing psychotropic medication. He did feel less anxious, but he thought that his concerns about side effects became linked with vague fears of being made even more ill by the medication, that is, that he might be poisoned. He both acknowledged and denied paranoid ideation. He used tranquilizers intermittently during the beginning of his analytic psychotherapy, but he gave up medication as the therapeutic relationship deepened and his symptoms diminished.

During his psychotherapy he was able to give a consistent, enlarging picture of his immediate family. His mother had only slowly recovered from severe postpartum depression after his birth, and he was actually cared for by his grandmother and a series of maids for the first 18 months of his life. His mother described herself as having had a nervous breakdown, but indicated that this was not helped by having a wanton, willful screaming infant. He was allowed to scream unless one of the mother-surrogates intervened, and he was then difficult to soothe. He remembered his mother as very high-strung and tense, self-centered and self-absorbed, temperamental and childish with rapid swings of mood and emotional lability. She was erratic in her thinking and feeling, officious while trying to be efficient and fastidious. Her frequent losses of temper were associated with verbal criticisms of the patient and slapping his face when she became agitated. He thought his mother's attentions and ambitions were more focused upon himself and that a peculiar interdependence had evolved. She was very ambitious for him and took pride in his accomplishment and intellectual skills. As he grew older, she became increasingly seductive, and in adolescence allowed him to see her undressed. He recalled earlier scenes of watching maids in various states of undress. When he became a physician, his mother brought him her complaints, expected him to do various tests, and finally, requested he do a complete physical examination, which might include a pelvic exam. She represented impaired regulation and stimulated conflict and regression. Their mutual seduction was also a source of unconscious guilt and expectation of punishment, merging with his paranoid attitudes.

It was then possible to further reconstruct the onset of his paranoid regression. His wife's visit to her gynecologist for a routine check-up had triggered renewed fantasies of her infidelity and betrayal, clearly linked to the incestuous seduction with his mother. The patient had acted this out in disguised form by having sexual relations with aides and nurses. He had tried sexual relations on an examining table, with incestuous and feminine unconscious implications. Stabbing pains in his heart were associated with stabbing his mother's veins to draw blood for chemical analysis. Oedipal guilt and fear of retaliation were important determinants in triggering the severe regressive escape from the dangers of castration and death by execution. With the onset of his brief delusion of being poisoned he had read about a rapist who died by hanging and had his last erection with his last breath.

The patient's father was described as good-natured, loquacious, but so devoted to his work that he was usually not physically or emotionally available. The parents frequently quarreled, alternating with reciprocal passive aggression. Both parents had mild somatic disorders, dishonest tendencies, and litigious attitudes. The patient tended to be hypochondriacal like his mother, with fears of many severe illnesses which included brain tumors. These personal worries were embedded in familial fears of illness and bodily attack. Dreams of decapitation were related to childhood traumata and intense castration anxiety, but also to fear of losing his head and going crazy. His castration threats had been intensified by operations on his penis for the removal of cysts and warts as an adult.

Of great importance, and reactivated in transference, was "brain illness," with episodes of coma as a result of a severe childhood illness. At 5 years of age the patient had developed an encephalitic episode and at 10 years of age he had an attack of meningitis. He had recovered rapidly, and there were no known organic sequellae. In his early teens he suffered an accidental eye injury with partial loss of vision. This was understood as castration and retaliation for his voyeurism, but was also associated with an inner vindictive attitude of "an eye for an eye." He had always had fantasies dating from early childhood of being an all-powerful avenger who could "get even" as well as dominate and subjugate imaginary adversaries. Illness, insult, and injury, and repeated trauma confirmed his persecutory and punitive fantasies.

After his eye injury the patient recalled the period of masturbation involving watching his mother, female relatives, and girls in class as well as calendar girls while he masturbated. He never had conscious homosexual fantasies or feelings. He was aware of identification with his mother as hypochondriacal, "thin-skinned," and prone to being hypercritical while unable to tolerate criticism. He could "dish out" criticism, but he couldn't take it. Unaware of his own femininity, he was, at the same time, cognizant of the exaggerated nature of his Don Juan compulsive promiscuity. Perhaps he needed to reassure himself about his masculinity, and his need to be in charge and control in all respects. Moreover, his wife's attitudes were not reassuring or soothing. She was frigid, ridiculed his sexual behavior, and once slapped his face during breast foreplay. This reminded him of his mother's inability to feed him, her slaps, and his underlying rage at and distrust of women. His wife's and his mother's criticism had been "poisonous," and while he was seductive like his mother, he had perhaps chosen his wife on the basis of certain opposite as well as similar characteristics. His affairs had always represented women who were all-giving for the moment without any demands or responsibilities for the patient. But the intense, compulsive search for one woman after the other in reality as well as fantasy was a type of frantic "erotomania."

Erotomania is the inverse of paranoia, in which erotic seduction defends against hate and rage. The erotomania, with its frantic passionate attachment, is the affective counterpart to ideas of reference. Passivity and homosexuality are also warded off, but a basic attachment to the dangerous inconstant object is sought, in fantasy, and after in action as well.

He could not find a solution to his ambivalence or the right close-ness to or distance from the partner. The relatively anonymous sexual encounter was like a "quick fix." He not only had immediate gratification but was comforted, consoled, and soothed. He associated to a fantasy of being "shot in the head" which again meant ejaculation and execution, but also brain injury, shooting heroin, and completely losing his mind. Perhaps he had somehow incorporated poisonous substances which could turn him from a frustrated and hungry childlike adult to a murderous madman!

As therapy progressed, his fears and his fantasies, his actual paranoia, rapidly subsided. He became far more confident about impulse control. The quarrels with his wife diminished in frequency and intensity, and he was able to reestablish a degree of stability in the marriage; his wife no longer pressed for divorce. His ego integration improved with the benefit of the therapeutic relationship, and the tie to his wife, the mother-surrogate, appeared to be maintained. He became considerably calmer and more reflective. He knew that medicine was a heavy burden as well as a peculiarly seductive and threatening situation for him. He then thought that clinical practice was not for him—he would be better off not treating patients; the patients would be better off without him; and he would have a better marriage without the headaches of direct patient care. He became aware of his jealousy of his wife and of her nurturing their children; she had postpartum depression, but he had unrecognized postpartum paranoia. He realized he would have better direction and control by not dashing about from patient to patient and affair to affair. His frantic and frenzied efforts to find a momentarily satisfying and soothing relationship had only resulted in increased disorganization, psychologically, and in his life in general. Yet, his psychic survival depended upon his restoration of object constancy and ego stability.

He would make the eventual decision to relinquish medicine in favor of research. And what research did he gravitate toward? He chose a research area in which part of his work prepared for testing the toxic and lethal dose of certain chemicals. This patient then manifested, in sequence, fears of being poisoned, poisoning patients, to the socially and scientifically acceptable poisoning of guineapigs. This was positive and progressive for the patient with rapid further remission of his paranoia. During the paranoid phase he was suspicious, watchful, and fearful of being scrutinized, jealous and fearful of being betrayed. With reintegration, he was no longer preoccupied with his addictive object hunger and "nursing grievances." His distrustful vigilance and hate could now be directed toward planning and execution of his research.

What can be inferred concerning the pathogenesis of this particular case of paranoid personality? The patient clearly showed the earmarks of intense oedipal conflict with associated oedipal rivalry and jealousy, positive and negative oedipal constellations, and regression under the sway of castration anxiety and oedipal guilt. His oedipal conflicts, however, and attempts at solution miscarried because of his severe regressive vulnerabilities. His oedipal organization was fragile, and his oedipal conflicts were infiltrated and permeated with narcissistic and preoedipal problems. There was a facade of phallic narcissism, manifested in his Don Juan behavior and exemplified in a fantasy of his penis becoming ever larger and leading to complete narcissistic satisfaction by sucking himself to orgasm. In this fantasy he was also both father and mother in the primal scene as well as mother and nursing infant. When regression set in it was a structural regression involving all agencies. Sadomasochistic object relations became more ambivalent, narcissistic, and incompletely differentiated. Castration anxiety was fused with separation anxiety. The patient omnipotently possessed the maternal narcissistic object in fantasy, thereby denying his need for her; or the object is devoured and eliminated in cycles of introjection and projection as the patient attempts to both preserve and destroy the disappointing narcissistic object. The devalued and despised narcissistic object is split or dissociated from the good, nurturing part object as described by Klein (1932).

The patient was the savior or rescuer Dr. Jekyll and the murderous Mr. Hyde. The fantasies of limitless gratification from the ever-bountiful part object or narcissistic object inevitably result in heightened ambivalence. It was not clear whether it was the narcissistic disorder or the unconscious conflicts, rage, and overwhelming anxiety that had impaired object constancy. This patient was unable to maintain an autonomous, stable, integrated mental representation of the object, and in degree of the self, irrespective of conflict and frustration (Mahler and Furer, 1968). The helter-skelter rushing toward and from narcissistic objects was not only defensive against incestuous and homosexual

110

oedipal passions, but probably represented ambivalence and regressive loss of object constancy. The instability of boundaries and defenses, and the appearance of delusions, pointed to a major early structural disturbance. Severe superego regression was associated with externalization of punishment onto archaic persecutory figures, a search for omnipotent, watchful protection, and the need for an external superego to set limits and maintain self-regulation. Superego externalization and the projection of blame and guilt in the paranoid personality is on a spectrum ranging from the well-organized and relatively realistic superego to archaic, fantastic, persecutory imagoes. These anlage and regressively transformed punitive and idealized superego components are more realistic and less primitive in the milder forms of paranoia. The degree of structural regression in these patients determines the likelihood of paranoid fantasy becoming paranoid behavior and the danger of malignant enactment.

The urge toward betrayal was matched by his jealousy and fears of betrayal. His reliance on projection, along with the pronounced narcissistic disorder and vulnerability, was consonant with the preoedipal disturbance which had not been successfully reorganized in the oedipal and postoedipal phases.

While Freud (1911) had emphasized pathognomonic repressed homosexuality in paranoia, he also noted the regression to narcissism. Schreber was both megalomanic and helplessly abused by God. At that time Freud did not explicitly consider that Schreber might actually have been an abused child, that there was historical truth in his delusion and that homosexual love and submission defended against hate and rage. In his later writings Freud emphasized initial aggressive dispositions, aggression toward the mother, sometimes associated with maternal aggression toward the infant during the preoedipal phase of development, and actual narcissistic injuries and threats to survival (Freud, 1923, 1931). Although Freud described preoedipal factors in female paranoia, his observations and those of analytic investigators who followed showed the applicability of preoedipal issues to a general theory of paranoia. Freud proposed that the preoedipal dread of being devoured by the mother was derived from hostility to the mother, often caused by her actual frustrating, restrictive, or seductive behavior. Immaturity and dependence on the mother favored hostility to her. The paranoid fear of being poisoned was connected by Freud with the traumatic experience of the birth of a sibling followed by the fantasy of

111

betrayal by the mother. The suspicion and accusations of the mother's faithlessness became elements imbued in the child's later paranoid character. The hostility and counterhostility of mother and child led to difficulties in comprehending the child's later Oedipus complex. Oedipal and preoedipal problems were fused and confused, and Freud (1931), at this point, cited a paranoid case of Mack-Brunswick's who had never developed beyond the preoedipal stage. As is so often the case in Freud studies, earlier and later formulations remain unintegrated.

The patient described here appears to have a history consistent with severe preoedipal disorder followed by seductive overstimulation and the equivalent of primal scene exposure. He was beset by feelings of injury, jealousy, exclusion, and betrayal related to the primal scene (Kanzer, 1952), but a primal scene suffused with preoedipal and narcissistic disorder. He lacked capacities for tenderness, intimacy, and truly warm, friendly relations and playfulness. Ambivalence endangered his capacity to love and be loved, and the enormous underlying rage threatened his destruction of self and object. The lack of object constancy is associated with a lack of ego integration, untamed infantile omnipotence, narcissistic regressive vulnerability, and underlying vulnerability to castration-separation panic and rage. It is postulated that the severe infantile difficulties during his first year and one-half of life, associated with his persistent screaming and continuing pathogenic object relations, contributed to his paranoid predisposition.

Paranoid patients may need protracted or intermittent treatment as well as a structured life situation to maintain ego integration and regain some basic trust (Erikson, 1950). This paranoid patient displayed, behind a social and professional veneer, the sexual promiscuity and ruthless exploitation of the narcissistic character; delusional fears of persecution, actual abuse of others, distrust, and the fear of betrayal by and actual betrayal of the object (Kernberg, 1975; Akhtar, 1990). The fragility, regressive, and aggressive loss of object constancy, and desperate attempts to regain or retain a constant object are very important determinants of paranoia. The reestablishment of a fragile object constancy is a progressive achievement which is related to recovery from paranoid regression. Our expanded and deeper understanding of the structure of paranoid psychopathology highlights the need for further research on the pathogenesis and treatment of these refractory, rigid personality disorders.

112

REFERENCES

Akhtar, S. (1990), Paranoid personality disorder: A synthesis. *Amer. J. Psychother.*, 44:5–25.

Blum, H. (1974), The borderline childhood of the Wolf Man. *J. Amer. Psychoanal. Assn.*, 22:721–742.

—— (1980), Paranoia and beating fantasy: An inquiry into the psychoanalytic theory of paranoia. *J. Amer. Psychoanal. Assn.*, 28:331–362.

—— (1981), Object inconstancy and paranoid conspiracy. *J. Amer. Psychoanal. Assn.*, 29:789–813.

Erikson, E. (1950), *Childhood and Society.* New York: W. W. Norton.

Freud, A. (1965), Normality and Pathology. *Writings*, Vol. 6. New York: International Universities Press.

Freud, S. (1911), Psycho-analytic notes on an autobiographical account of a case of paranoia (dementia paranoides). *Standard Edition*, 12:3–79. London: Hogarth Press, 1958.

—— (1918), From the History of an Infantile Neurosis. *Standard Edition*, 17:3–122. London: Hogarth Press, 1955.

—— (1922), Some neurotic mechanisms in jealousy, paranoia and homosexuality. *Standard Edition*, 18:221–231. London: Hogarth Press, 1955.

—— (1923), The Ego and the Id. *Standard Edition*, 19:3–59. London: Hogarth Press, 1961.

—— (1931), Female sexuality. *Standard Edition*, 21:223–243. London: Hogarth Press, 1961.

—— (1937), Constructions in analysis. *Standard Edition*, 23:255–269. London: Hogarth Press, 1964.

Frosch, J. (1990), *Psychodynamic Psychiatry*, Vol. 2. New York: International Universities Press.

Kanzer, M. (1952), Manic-depressive psychoses with paranoid tendencies. *Internat. J. Psycho-Anal.*, 33:34–42.

Kernberg, O. (1975), *Borderline Conditions and Pathological Narcissism.* New York: Jason Aronson.

Klein, M. (1932), *The Psycho-Analysis of Children.* New York: Norton.

Kohut, H. (1972), Thoughts on narcissism and narcissistic rage. *The Psychoanalytic Study of the Child*, 27:367–400. Chicago: Quadrangle.

Mahler, M. (1971), A study of the separation-individuation process and its possible application to borderline phenomena in the psychoanalytic situation. *The Psychoanalytic Study of the Child*, 26:403–424. Chicago: Quadrangle.

———— Furer, E. (1968), *On Human Symbiosis and the Vicissitudes of Individuation*. New York: International Universities Press.

McDevitt, J. (1975), Separation-individuation and object constancy. *J. Amer. Psychoanal. Assn.*, 23:713–742.

Meissner, W. (1978), *The Paranoid Process*. New York: Jason Aronson.

Socarides, C. (1966), On vengeance. *J. Amer. Psychoanal. Assn.*, 14:356–375.

8

Lovesickness

Arnold Goldberg, M.D.

Being sick with love in some way touches us all. Though many may claim to have escaped the malady themselves, we are surrounded by examples of the ailment in poetry, novels, movies, and song. But true and lasting lovesickness is never a flirtation with the virus; rather it is an all-consuming, painful, oppressive feeling that possesses its victims and renders them as marionettes to the puppeteer of Eros. It ranges from the mildest form of short-lived infatuation or puppy love, on the one hand, to the erotomania of Kraepelin and de Clerambault (Segal, 1989). It is a syndrome whose hallmark is a systematized delusion of being convinced of the passionate love of another person. Points on the spectrum are often characterized as being illnesses when spoken of as being "sick with love," and, of late, one endpoint has become a bona fide member of the psychiatric book of illnesses, DSM-III-R, where it joins a group of delusional (paranoid) disorders (APA, 1987). It here qualifies perhaps as an example of the extreme in the continuum of lovesickness. That it is an illness that cannot be ignored or tolerated and lived with is clear, inasmuch as it usually subordinates the conduct of ordinary life to its demands. And interestingly and perhaps most peculiarly, there is no agreement of any sort as to its treatment or cure, although there is a surprising consensus that one either overcomes it or one submits to it, or else it magically goes away by itself. What to do until that desired and unhurried resolution comes about is a matter for folklore which encompasses an extraordinary number of experts and advice. Yet the most surprising contrast to that plethora of cures is that single voice of the varied victims: there is but one cure to lovesickness, and it is that of love. They are all convinced of that.

PSYCHIATRIC LITERATURE

The focus of this brief review will be on the particular group of disorders of love characterized by the symptom of erotomania, which is said to be the delusional belief that one is passionately loved by another. A recent revisiting of this symptom by psychiatric investigators has prompted a new concern for its status in terms of diagnosis and clinical course. Whereas it is seen by some to be a singular delusion "in its own right" (Rudden, Sweeney, and Frances, 1990, p. 625) some claim it as related to paranoia, some to schizophrenia, and some to affective disorders. The claim that it is most prevalent in women is disputed by some authors but usually there is felt to be around a 75 percent female predominance. In men there seems to be a variation which is sometimes termed borderline erotomania, wherein the man is in the grips of an intense attachment to an unrequited love. Though the argument about what is the best term for this variation of the symptom, ranging from obsessive love to nondelusional erotomania, remains unresolved, there is agreement that it may itself be a rather widespread malady (Meloy, 1990).

There is likewise a range of opinions as to the clinical course and advised treatment for this symptom or symptom complex. The usual feeling is that it is most refractory to treatment, but this is somewhat tempered by some reports of a subgroup of patients who are said to have a better clinical course with fewer hospitalizations (Rudden et al., 1990, p. 627). Treatment is said to range from lithium to what can only be called unspecified intervention (p. 626) since no details are given as to exactly what is done to or with the patients.

This last point seems to be rather representative of the psychiatric literature, which is clearly concerned with classification of the disorder and sometimes with its management. That psychiatrists in the 1990s would concern themselves with what are essentially trivial exercises in arrangement, while seemingly oblivious of Freud's elegant explanation of just where erotomania falls in relation to paranoia, is surely a cause for despair. Freud's variations on the theme of "I love him" elaborated upon the Schreber case (Freud, 1911) were used to explain erotomania following the formula, "I do not love him, I love her, because she loves me." The intense attachment of a male for a woman is but a further variation on the formula, and, although it was still felt to stem from the male patient's homosexual longings, there seems no need to separate the delusion of being loved from that of insisting upon another's love, save for the step that brings one closer to psychosis. Indeed as Fenichel (1945, p. 432) says, the man who projects his exaggerated desire for an object onto a woman is truly "persecuted with love."

PSYCHOANALYTIC LITERATURE REVIEW

To accurately and honestly review a psychoanalytic literature on lovesickness requires that first we know something of what is said about love, which is surprisingly little. It is as though love remains outside of psychopathology, with the most obvious explanation being that no one complains of it unless and until it becomes a sickness. One exception is Kernberg (1974b) who presents both a developmental schema for being able to fall in love as well as a description of the characteristics of mature love. His first is based on the full development of oral and body-surface erotism and its integration into total object relations. Here he echoes Winnicott's prerequisite for the development of the capacity for concern. Kernberg's second presentation lists mature love as consisting of the sum of the initial capacity to fall in love, the ability to be tender, to have a sophisticated idealization, and to have attained the capacity for identification and empathy with the love object. The consecutive stages of development of internalized object relations carry the foundation for this descriptive, clinical assessment. Kernberg's own review of the literature reflects the paucity of contributions by psychoanalysts to the subject, but one is well served by the works of Bergmann (1971), Josselyn (1971), and Bak (1973), all of whom connect the capacity to love to that of being able to experience depression and to mourn. Mature love lies on a developmental line directed toward achieving that capacity.

Therefore loving is a capacity, an achievement, a mark of growth and maturity. Narcissistic, borderline, primitive patients may have sexual relations, idealized relations, and even stable relations but they do not have "true love." Balint (1948) says that the latter includes idealization, tenderness, and a special form of identification. Fenichel (1945) tells us that one can speak of love only when one's own satisfaction is impossible to achieve without that of satisfying the object as well (p. 84). On the whole, while the true nature of love may elude psychoanalysis, as in Fenichel's saying that we know nothing about the specific nature "of the identification in love," there is no lack of authoritative statements about the psychopathology of love, and to that we turn and so to an abundance of contributions.

Persons who need to feel love but cannot love actively are considered to be "love addicts" (Fenichel, 1945, p. 387). They are described as inconsiderate people who demand that others "understand" their feelings. The origin of what is termed "an archaic type of self-esteem regulation" (Fenichel, 1945, p. 388) is said to come from a wish to regain the feeling of infantile omnipotence by a projection of it onto parents and thereupon participating in the parental omnipotence. Such participation is said to be the feeling of being loved. If one is overly narcissistic then the need for self-love overshadows love for the other. A higher postnarcissistic love occurs with the capacity for object love and thus a new self-respect emerges (Fenichel, 1945, p. 85). It seems that narcissism is what we must study in order to better understand lovesickness.

Victor Tausk (1933) discussed the early stages of narcissism characterized by absolute self-satisfaction without others and without a world. He felt that this innate narcissism is followed by a pathological feeling of estrangement and then a projection of this discomfort onto the outer world. A subsequent sense of persecution may be formed by the construction of an influencing machine which is a summation of some or all of the pathology projected outward. This machine represents a projection of the entire body. It controls, regulates, and may exploit the person. Kohut (1972) has elaborated this scheme by considering the machine as an early, albeit pathological phase in the development of the idealized parental imago, a stage in a developmental line of narcissism. For most analytic writers, lovesickness is a pathological condition related to early difficulties in the deployment of narcissistic concerns. Whether one believes that true love goes beyond narcissism or else is a manifestation of more mature narcissism, it seems that there is a consensus of feeling that archaic or primitive narcissism is held responsible for the difficulties in love: those that range from being possessed by love in erotomania to the excessive idealization that accompanies ordinary love (Spruiell, 1979).

Freud felt that being in love consisted in a flowing over of libido onto the object, and that in many forms of love-choice the object serves as a substitute for some unattained ideal of our own. "We love it on account of the perfections which we have striven to reach for our own ego, and which we should now like to procure in this roundabout way as a means of satisfying our narcissism" (Freud, 1922, pp. 112–113). Thus we love both to fulfill ourselves and to heal ourselves. Indeed it seems to be that we use love as a balm and a cure, even if it not be that "true" state that seems so elusive.

The sequence of perfect self-love, followed by some sort of pain or discomfort which is projected outward, is then resolved in the form of the sought-for love object which is seen as the source of peace and pleasure. This object can be persecutory as well; but, at heart, the longed for object is always a bit of the long lost perfection of the self. Thus it is always narcissistic, and its attainment leads to perfect bliss. It need have no special properties of its own since it fundamentally is the self. For Tausk it was often a representation of the genitals, and the hurtful machines were embodiments of genital irritation. The particular ingredients of the initial pain and the subsequent cure vary over a wide range of incidents and persons, but the basic ingredient is that of narcissistic injury; and the basic cure is a balm to the self.

The clinical material which follows will aim to show a range of the pathology of love sickness as well as a range of therapy. The treatment covers both psychotherapy and psychoanalysis and demonstrates an earlier thesis (Goldberg, 1981) that points out the distinction between the two. It is perhaps most unfortunate that more recent psychiatric writing (Segal, 1989) on the subject gives little attention to the treatment of this malady. But surely, without an extensive study of the underlying developmental pathology, psychiatry will always have to rest content between the poles of description and pharmacology. Psychiatry today is becoming estranged from psychology.

In our first case a demonstration of the treatment of lovesickness which involves a repair of an injured self will be presented. Such cases of psychotherapy are regularly no more than educated hunches about etiology and cure, inasmuch as a well-developed transference cannot be studied and resolved in most treatments. If one turns to a more in-depth psychoanalytic pursuit, an opportunity is offered to make more meaningful generalizations about the psychopathology of this or any other malady. Psychoanalysis involves a more profound reorganization of the personality, and the process allows one to scrutinize the development of the transference and its resolution in some detail. Though these two patients may share a common symptom, it is not the intent of this essay to compare them much at all in terms of their diagnosis and course of treatment. It would be unfortunate to try to exchange the concepts of these patients beyond the commonality of symptom and some general ideas about the dynamics of its origin.

CLINICAL EXAMPLE

The patient is a professional man in his late twenties who comes to see a psychiatrist because he is hopelessly in love with a woman who seems to care little for him but whose psychic presence dominates almost every moment of his waking life. He tells me, the psychiatrist, that he is agitated and depressed and can only contemplate feeling better once he has obtained the love of his beloved. This woman is difficult for me to imagine, since he has little to actually say about her. He has seen her only a few times and never has been on terms that one would consider intimate with her. He insists that she satisfies all of his "specs" for a woman, a list that seems primarily devoted to physical attributes. Indeed he wants only to talk about her, and to figure her out, to gain advice and reassurance as to how to have her with but secondary recognition that perhaps his supposed love is exaggerated and unreal. At no time, however, does he or can he conceal his intense psychological pain.

The patient has little to say about his past except that such sweeping states of love have overcome him on previous occasions. Though he insists that this one is different and special, he feels that he is especially prone to falling in love with a rather similar sort of woman, that is, one who is physically appealing and about whom he knows relatively little. This latest episode was connected in time to the death of his father. He says he could not be sure if he was depressed because of grief over that death or because of unhappiness over his unrequited love. But certainly he can and does talk incessantly about his longed-for love while having very little to say about his lost parent.

He comes for treatment upon the advice of friends, but admits that he has seen other therapists both some time ago while in college and most recently as he has shopped around for the right person. He picks me, and I feel pleased at winning the lottery. But as this treatment, a twice per week, face-to-face arrangement proceeds, I find him terribly boring and frustrating. I never seem to know what is happening in his life which seems shallow and empty, although lots of people are mentioned as passing through it. But his love dominates everything. The unloved lover occasionally talks to his paramour on the telephone, but she is cool and careful not to give him any hope or encouragement. He wants only to marry and has made elaborate plans for their future together. At times I think that this is so close to a delusion, that I fear he cannot ever be disabused of this intense passion. He compares himself to John Hinckley and his obsession with Jodie Foster, but immediately insists that he is different, since he really feels he knows this person, and his love is genuine. One day he manages to meet and talk to someone who has dated this woman whom he loves and next he tells me a dream: he is flying and being chased by helicopters. He is frightened but suddenly manages to be free of them, and he is soaring. He feels wonderful in the dream and recounts his conviction that he is every bit as good as this other man and so is convinced that he will be able to succeed in winning his love.

However, such moments of pleasure are rare, since he is usually miserable. The phone is his only contact with this woman, and he comes to fear it and then becomes captured by it. Finally he manages to get his beloved to agree to see him; and so he decides to propose. I sit in amazement as he tells me of an elaborate arrangement involving dinner, music, a proposal, and presentation of a ring. I try gently to tell him that this is really a first date, even though he may feel it to be the fulfillment of a life's dream. My wish to be a calm and rational presence is probably somewhat betrayed by the absolute dumbfounded-ness that accompanies my comments, but my amazement that ushered in this hour is intensified as he then agrees with me. And once again

I feel that there is a part of him that is sane and tied to reality that sits apart from and watches the incredible scene unfold.

My therapeutic tactic is a simple one, as I ask that he tells me what actually goes on in his life, so that I can connect these real events with the fantastic flight to the dreams of his loved one. They do go out. They do not seem to have a very good time, and she seems not to be a very nice person, but his love continues unabated. He tells a dream of oral sex in which tentacles of her vagina extend out to entangle and capture him, and he is in a state of bliss. And I am disheartened.

He continues his hot pursuit of this woman until she very clearly tells him that there is no future for them. She says to him: "You've made me up." He is devastated and talks of suicide. He resolves not to see her (an easy resolution and one he makes fairly frequently since he never succeeds in its achievement anyway) nor to call her. And for a short while he says he feels better and describes a lifting of his depression. But not for very long. Yet during the interlude he manages to tell me a little of his early life: one dominated by a stern and demanding father and a compliant and pleasing mother. Father was a perfectionist. He came every night to a dinner painstakingly prepared by mother who was inevitably crestfallen as her husband managed to discover some flaw and to become angry. The patient joined in this effort to please this irascible man, and felt that he succeeded but rarely. He sees himself now as someone who tried very hard to be perfect. His fondest pursuit was of mechanical drawing: a labor that led to absolutely perfect constructions. He has no difficulty at all in claiming that his longed-for love is the true embodiment of perfection, nor that their union would capture that elusive state in a permanent form for him.

As he speaks more of his father there are many positive memories as well, while those of his mother seem more elusive and vague. And as the treatment proceeds, he clearly charges me with the task of being the perfect person: one who will magically cure him. And this reference to a magical cure is more than a figure of speech, since he unhesitantly wants me to say something that will make him all better, to "figure it out" so that he is once again happy. But his past life reveals little such enduring experience, since he now occasionally remembers thinking of suicide in high school and periodic depressions. He reports a heavy use of marijuana in his teens and occasional use of it, cocaine, and angel dust, at present. His self-medication is rarely successful, and he counts more and more on therapy.

After about six months of treatment the patient is able to recount a coherent story of his activities, and we are able to pinpoint the turning of his mind to his beloved at distinct moments of loneliness, hurt feelings, or feeling personally inadequate. It is really only at these times that I am somewhat lifted to a state of interested involvement, since much of the other portion of the therapy consists of his struggle to understand the woman and his asking me whether I am paying attention and whether I can tell him if he will soon be better. I often share his bewilderment and befuddlement.

And better indeed he slowly becomes. He begins to stay away from her, from calling her, and planning to be with her, and he has moments of relief. It is of some interest that his periods of relief are described as being equivalent to those rare moments when he felt he did or could or would have her. Love here seems to take the form of peace and contentment rather than ecstasy and fulfillment. It is more of a balm than a peak experience.

The treatment was planned to be limited to one year, and, as the end of that period approaches, the patient has to make plans to move to a new position in a different city. His condition worsens over the prospect of leaving, and he becomes more dependent and begins to talk about suicide. As the delusional quality of his lost love has dissipated, the inevitable confrontation with reality has become overwhelming. He feels lost and empty. He is not up to the demands of his new job. He says that he has learned nothing in his training and needs to begin again to take in everything that he needs to know. I think of a child who has failed to fill in all of the details of growing up with an idealizable parent and who therefore has to gulp it all down in one fell swoop; a child lacking in essential psychological structure. His leaving his therapy is more than he can handle, and during a visit home, he is hospitalized for a week. He speaks to me on the phone, is soon discharged, and returns to treatment. He has decided to move on to the new city and sounds reasonable and less depressed, although he claims to be very anxious every morning upon awakening. We see each other until he leaves. He discontinues the medication given to him in the hospital with no difficulty. He calls me from the new place and sounds as good as he has been, and now decides to continue treatment with someone there. I feel less worried about him and begin to think that, at a minimum, his lovesickness is cured.

THE THEORY OF THE TECHNIQUE

The patient can easily and readily see himself as a love addict for whom a "fix" is equivalent to a connection to the very person of his beloved. But the mere knowledge of this fact is of little more use to him in curing his addiction than knowing one needs heroin is of aid to that sort of addict. Rather we posit a specific form of healing that takes place in this patient; a healing of his psyche that has to do with the concept of a split, in this case, a vertical split.

Kohut postulated the vertical split as a division in the psyche between the reality ego and a portion of the ego that is disavowed. That latter portion is split away from reality and proceeds to react with the world in a manner that gratifies archaic, narcissistic demands with little heed for control or neutralization. Primitive exhibitionistic or childlike merger wishes dominate the psyche and seek out the relationships that fulfill such infantile needs. The free expression of otherwise forbidden, that is, unconscious or repressed wishes, can only take place by way of a portion of the psyche that is not under the control of the reality principle. It does so episodically and periodically in some forms of narcissism such as perversions, and it does so regularly in other forms such as psychosis. Treatment of all such disorders involves an appeal to the reality ego and a healing of the vertical split. This healing or repair of a disjunction in the psyche is not itself, however, accomplished by an appeal to reason or an insistence on denying the irrational. Rather it comes about by offering the patient another outlet for these archaic fantasies: one that both gratifies and controls, and is ultimately under the sway of the reality ego.

The dominance of the reality ego must be achieved without sacrificing the energies offered by the primitive wishes and fantasies. We see the patient's despair and depression that follows from the abandonment of his quasi-delusional state, with no hope for the achievement of the always sought for bliss and redemption. Thus it follows naturally that the confrontation with reality guarantees that all is lost, and so this state is necessarily disavowed. Only an activation of a selfobject that allows for the absorption of these archaic narcissistic fantasies is of use to the patient. As the analyst or therapist becomes available for, in this case, an idealized selfobject, the patient redirects his fantasies in the transference, and here it is necessary to emphasize that this is not a transference of object-directed love but rather one of narcissistic form. This selfobject attachment becomes available and also allows for the repair of the vertical split, since treatment directs attention by way of the reality ego to the here and now of the transference. Thus, this psychotherapy is essentially one of a repair to a damaged self.

It remains to be seen whether a similar sort of dynamic is evident in other forms of lovesickness, and it remains a question as to whether or not such a hypothetical consideration of the pathology is substantiated by the reconstructions offered in an analysis. We next turn to such an effect with a similar sort of symptom.

CLINICAL EXAMPLE

This second patient is a 42-year-old professional man who is married but who has been a Don Juan for much of his life and has remained so throughout his marriage of five years. He says that he is fairly happy with his wife who is described as the only woman he has ever met of whom he does not tire. He continually contemplates and considers divorce, however, because of their failure to have children, coupled with his own feeling that life will be incomplete without a child of his own. Marriage and occasional sexual escapades are not the whole of this patient's love life, which has been also punctuated by episodes of extreme and overwhelming love for certain women. He says that this sort of love is in no way similar to the love he has for his wife or his other bedpartners, but rather is an all-consuming preoccupation with these women with whom he falls in love, usually without knowing them at all. He becomes totally devoted to a pursuit of such a woman and this occupies all of his waking hours. He is sick with love and is only relieved when he can spend time with his beloved. This sort of head-over-heels falling in love has occurred periodically from adolescence to the present time and is the immediate cause for his seeking psychoanalysis. He has had one or two or three previous psychotherapies, but he says that they amounted to little more than support. The uncertainty of the number is based upon the statement he recalls from his first course of treatment. The therapist said that he thought the patient was a pleasant person, but he knew him not at all. The last and referring therapist joined in this appraisal of the patient as an enigma. No one knows him, and his treatments do not amount to much.

The history of the patient seems uneventful, since he describes himself as never getting too interested or involved in anything. His mother is described as sweet and simple; his deceased father as someone he was very fond of but rarely had much to say to; his sister as a nice person who lives in another state and with whom he speaks about once a year. The patient is successful in his work, but it seems a labor of superficial contacts and conclusions. Indeed the patient is quick to characterize himself as being superficial; someone not interested in very many things including the many women of his life, with the singular exception of his wife. The periodic ones who inhabit the world of overwhelming love are more objects of pain than of interest.

The women of this man's lovesickness are usually very striking but difficult people. He absolutely adores them and uniformly discovers that they are untrustworthy or inconsiderate or downright cruel. He pursues them with a passion that does not spend itself even when he discovers their very obvious flaws. He often falls out of love just as quickly as he managed to arrive upon the scene, but this reversal is usually after many months of heartache and disappointment accompanied by a blindness to these failings of his paramour, since the cessation of his lovesickness seems not to be caused by a recognition of being mistreated. Rather it happens suddenly and inexplicably and is peculiarly complete and absolute. He cares not a whit for them after it ends.

He says that he put these particular women on a pedestal in that they "allowed" him to go to bed with them. This meant to him that they cared, but he learned later that this was not true. Eventually he learned the truth about these women, but usually long after he had been manipulated and used. Much of the beginning of this patient's treatment was devoted to a detailed accounting of his relationships with the various "loves" of his life; uniformly they turned out to be less than admirable persons. His treatment, in fact, was initiated when he was in the throes of a cycle of lovesickness and was advised by a previous therapist to undergo psychoanalysis. He followed this advice, began an analysis, and very soon thereafter lost interest in this woman.

Indeed his analysis is characterized by an absence of lovesickness as well as a steady diminution in his philandering.

Another feature that dominated much of the early period of analysis was his justified claim to being a man of virtue. While seemingly surrounded by colleagues who were unreliable, untrustworthy, and uncaring of their fellow men, my patient insisted upon living a life of honesty, integrity, and reliability. He was known as someone who never cheated or cared overly much about money, who always kept his word, who could be called upon at any time to fulfill a task, and who constantly served as an ideal to younger men. Much of his early hours were spent in delineating and distancing himself from scoundrels of various kinds, and there never was a hint of this being anything but genuine. He confessed that it seemed ridiculous to him that he could lay claim to being possessed of such high ideals while he had little or no compunction about cheating on his wife. Thus the disparity or the split in the psychological arena of ideals and values was clearly demonstrated and presented by the patient.

The other striking phenomenon of this analysis was the gradual reappearance in dreams of the father; a man who became a cardiac cripple when the patient was 10 years old. As father again became alive and real, the patient had a series of dreams about something missing. This was best seen in a dream of a hernia repair which did not have enough tissue to cover the wound. It was seen in the transference by a chronic inability to come for full sessions in all of the appointed hours. It was seen in the associations by his insistence that there was nothing deep to be discovered within him. The latter protests were met by my pursuit of this as a defense against underlying painful issues. I early felt that his conflicts lay beneath this defense of superficiality.

We are told (Coen, 1986; LeFarge, 1989) to be wary of patients who present themselves as being defective psychologically or who complain of emptiness, inasmuch as each of these presentations may hide destructive and sexual wishes. We are even asked (Weinshel, 1990) to cease our debate upon the conflict versus deficit issue in psychoanalysis. The ever-present skepticism of the analyst seems peculiarly designed by some to believe in certain issues without doubt, and also to doubt certain issues without a chance of belief. But, wittingly or otherwise, my patient felt empty and dreamt of defects, and my skepticism came to naught. A telling example of the reality of his emptiness came when the subject of "something missing" was considered by him. He said that he had a very strong emotional bond with his father but always felt that he did not get enough from him. Just what he did not get seemed primarily to focus upon knowing about and being interested in things. He is just like his dad: he has no interests. Father was a gambler who played cards whenever he was not working. When he went on vacation, he played cards; when he got home from work he played cards, and when he was very ill from heart disease he had time only for cards. Although father sounded like a sad person to me, my patient said he seemed more bored than sad. They rarely spoke to one another, and once when the son asked the father why he had stayed in what seemed to be an unhappy marriage, he was told that sometimes it was better to put up with things. Though my patient also gambled on occasion he hardly qualified as a pathological gambler, as was his father; and although he lacked interest in things he was rarely bored as much as he was restless and discontented. His chronicle of life's activities was one of a busy person who did all the right things, was liked and appreciated and even admired by colleagues and friends, who was a constant and reliable friend and family man, but who felt dissatisfied, empty, and unfulfilled. For him there were no real pleasures in life save for episodic sexual exploits and periodic longings for a woman with whom he fell in love. As analysis proceeded we came upon the empty depression that underlay these symptoms. He came more regularly, he felt connected, all the while claiming that he had nothing to say, and he confronted the intense feeling of running in place with no real feeling of accomplishment or fulfillment. Falling in love was a quick fix and a sure cure. Psychoanalysis was a process of structural reorganization which allowed for a filling-in of the missing aspects of the idealized selfobject: the father who was equally empty and hidden from view.

SEXUALIZATION

We speak of sexualization when an activity or a function has an increased erogenicity. Freud said that an organ that is sexualized behaves like a cook who no longer wants to work in the kitchen when she and the master of the house are having a love affair, when he referred to the sexualization of a nonsexual activity (Fenichel, 1945, p. 179). We speak of pseudosexuality when acts that are apparently sexual serve defensive purposes. Prevailing narcissistic aims may disturb what is felt to be genuine sexuality, and it is said (Fenichel, 1945, p. 516) that one can readily differentiate between reactive sexuality which has underlying anxiety and genuine sexuality. It is claimed as well, however, that these narcissistic needs of patients can lay no claim to being inborn "true instincts" in contrast to sexuality, and ultimately they must be analyzed in terms of the vicissitudes of early instinctual conflicts.

If we put aside this dogged insistence on the genuine conflicts that underlie narcissistic pathology, we can reexamine the concept of the sexualization of the narcissistic relationship. It is clearly seen as an effort to retain the linkage to the narcissistic object; that is, the selfobject through a participation in sexual activity which may have a variety of manifestations and either perverse or fairly normal appearing. It may also be classified as pseudosexuality, however, since it is in the service of holding on to the selfobject and thus warding off the empty depression or impending anxiety of fragmentation. In excess it may be seen as an effort to thwart the regressive moves of selfobject loss, but it may be profitable to bear in mind that all love relationships carry an element of the nongenuine or pseudosexual within them. Sexualization of narcissistic objects brings sexual activity to an arena that is not properly sexual, and when subjected to analysis allows one to see the nonsexual components of the function: in this case, a relationship to a selfobject. The analysis likewise exposes the usually painful affective states which lie beneath the sexuality and which initiate the activity when their imminent appearance is signaled. The sexualized selfobject halts the regression, handles the painful affect states, allows for an experience of mastery, and may even heighten self-esteem. No wonder that it lays claim to incredible healing powers and little wonder that its absence is a sickness. But its regular betrayal of reality necessarily leads to an accompanying cost to adequate adaptation to the world since, as Glover (1933) first noted, most perversions follow the rule of fetishism wherein a truth known by one part of the personality must be split off and denied by another part. Glover's thesis is echoed in Kohut, and both claim a defect in perversions that does not follow the singularity of oedipal conflicts but rather lies in a rent in the fabric of the ego: a defect, once again, of psychic structure.

DISCUSSION

Imagine if you will a line of narcissism that claims attachment to an object, in this case an idealized one but without a sexual component. The earliest stages are those of archaic merger that may indeed manifest a pathological stage akin to Tausk's influencing machine. Later stages involving the mental mechanisms that Freud suggested allow us to envision the symptoms of intense idealization, intense longing, and intense watchfulness, or variations thereof. All of these stages deserve the appellation of narcissistic inasmuch as these objects are necessary, indeed vital, aspects of survival, and they have no real individuality. They are selfobjects. It is easy to say that one loves them or needs them or is tormented by them. Adding a sexual component is a convenient and clever way to increase their social acceptance as well as to master anxiety. This is the mistake made in assigning paranoia to a homosexual conflict. Rather it is a narcissistic problem which may or may not be sexualized, and the latter, on occasion, is of homosexual content. Psychoanalysis reverses the process and one sees the desexualization, the change from outer to inner torment, and then the establishment of a stable configuration that lends aspects of peace and bliss to the defective patient. But it should be clear that there are no deeper sexual conflicts to be unearthed save as we insist upon them. These are not cases of love that has gone astray but rather are those of pathological selfobject relationships become sexualized. Of course, treatment is well-nigh impossible without an analytic entry point to understanding the disorder, and if this is not available then busying oneself with classification is probably the best one can hope for.

Cases of lovesickness are misnomers. They belong less to the category of love, whatever that may be, and more to that of narcissistic imbalance. It may well be the case that all love is a mixture of both, and "true" love may or may not claim less of narcissism than that experienced by most of us. But just as we must reexamine true love, so must we look again at the sexual component, since the same dilemma comes at the point of distinguishing genuine from reactive sexuality. Since a good deal of sexuality is reactive, it is necessary to recognize that the underlying narcissistic needs of the sexual act can be seen as either primitive or mature in nature. True love and true sex may well be able to be narcissistic. It should come as no surprise to realize that we may have had little to say about lovesickness, because we came upon it without a proper guide. To see it as a sickness of the self is the royal road to the proper treatment of this malady of unhappiness.

CONCLUSION

Lovesickness spans a range of disorders from the early infatuations of adolescence to the malignant form of delusional erotomania. The spectrum covers not the vicissitudes of sexual or object love but rather those of narcissism. The latter developmentally shows a parallel range from archaic, primitive selfobject relationships to mature ones. This line of development points out the places of these disorders from mild to severe. It bespeaks a defect in psychic structure accompanied by a split in the personality: a split of reality rather than of repression. Psychotherapy repairs the damaged self; psychoanalysis reorganizes it, and both are effective if properly applied in cases of lovesickness.

REFERENCES

American Psychiatric Association (1987), *Diagnostic and Statistical Manual of Mental Disorders*, 3rd ed. rev. (DSM-III-R). Washington, DC: American Psychiatric Press.

Bak, R. C. (1973), Being in love and object loss. *Internat. J. Psycho-Anal.*, 54:1–8.

Balint, M. (1948), On genital love. In: *Primary Love and Psychoanalytic Technique*. London: Tavistock, pp. 109–120.

Bergmann, M. S. (1971), Psychoanalytic observations on the capacity to love. In: *Separation-Individuation*, ed. J. B. McDevitt & C. F. Settlage. New York: International Universities Press, pp. 15–40.

Coen, S. J. (1986), The sense of defect. *J. Amer. Psychoanal. Assn.*, 34:47–68.

Fenichel, O. (1945), *The Psychoanalytic Theory of Neuroses*. New York: W. W. Norton.

Freud, S. (1911), Psycho-analytic notes on an autobiographical account of a case of paranoia (dementia paranoides). *Standard Edition*, 12:3–79. London: Hogarth Press, 1958.

———— (1922), Group psychology and the analysis of the ego. *Standard Edition*, 18:69–143. London: Hogarth Press, 1955.

Glover, E. (1933), The relation of perversion formation to the development of the reality sense. *Internat. J. Psycho-Anal.*, 14:486–504.

Goldberg, A. (1981), Self psychology and the distinctiveness of psychotherapy. *Internat. J. Psychoanal. Psychother.*, 8:57–70.

Josselyn, I. (1971), The capacity to love: A possible reformation. *J. Amer. Acad. Child Psychiatry*, 10:6–22.

Kernberg, O. F. (1974a), Barriers to falling and remaining in love. *J. Amer. Psychoanal. Assn.*, 22:486–511.

———— (1974b), Mature love: Prerequisites and characteristics. *J. Amer. Psychoanal. Assn.*, 22:743–768.

Kohut, H. (1972), *The Analysis of the Self*. New York: International Universities Press.

LaFarge, L. (1989), Emptiness as defense in severe regressive states. *J. Amer. Psychoanal. Assn.*, 37:965–996.

Meloy, J. R. (1990), Nondelusional or borderline erotomania. *Amer. J. Psychiatry*, 147:820–824.

Rudden, M., Sweeney, J. & Frances, A. (1990), Diagnosis and clinical course of erotomania and other delusional patients. *Amer. J. Psychiatry*, 147:625–628.

Segal, J. (1989), Erotomania revisited: From Kraepelin to DSM-III-R. *Amer. J. Psychiatry*, 146:1261–1266.

Spruiell, V. (1979), Freud's concepts of idealization. *Psychoanal. Quart.*, 27:777–791.

Tausk, V. (1933), On the origin of the "Influencing Machine" in schizophrenia. *Psychoanal. Quart.*, 2:519–556.

Weinshel, E. (1990), How wide is the widening scope of psychoanalysis and how solid is its structural model? *J. Amer. Psychoanal. Assn.*, 38:275–295.

9

Paranoia: A Part of Every Analysis

Arnold M. Cooper, M.D.

Franz Kafka, an expert on paranoia, gave a vivid description of some of the characteristics of the paranoid personality in his story "The Burrow" (1923 to 1924). The story is a first person account by an unidentified creature which describes the construction of its hidden underground burrow. I shall quote some excerpts from the beginning of the story.

> I have completed the construction of my burrow and it seems to be successful. All that can be seen from outside is a big hole; that, however, really leads nowhere. . . . True, some ruses are so subtle that they defeat themselves, I know that better than anyone. . . . But you do not know me if you think I am afraid, or that I built my burrow simply out of fear . . . someone could step on the moss or break through it, and then my burrow would lie open, and anybody who liked—please note, however, that quite uncommon abilities would also be required—could make his way in and destroy everything for good. I know

A slightly different version of this chapter appeared in the *Journal of the American Psychoanalytic Association*, Volume 41, Number 2, 1993. It is reprinted here with the permission of the editor.

that very well and even now, at the zenith of my life, I can scarcely pass an hour in complete tranquility . . . in my dreams I often see a greedy muzzle sniffing around it persistently. . . . [P]rudence itself demands that I should have a way of leaving at a moment's notice if necessary, prudence itself demands, as alas! so often, to risk one's life. All this involves very laborious calculations, and the sheer pleasure of the mind in its own keenness is often the sole reason why one keeps it up. I must have a way of leaving at a moment's notice, for, despite all my vigilance, may I not be attacked from some quite unexpected quarter? . . . . I certainly have the advantage of being in my own house and knowing all the passages and how they run. A robber may very easily become my victim and a succulent one, too. . . . And it is not only by external enemies that I am threatened. There are also enemies in the bowels of the earth. I have never seen them, but legend tells of them and I firmly believe in them. . . . But the most beautiful thing about my burrow is the stillness. Of course, that is deceptive. At any moment it may be shattered and then all will be over [pp. 325–327].

The creature describes the center of his burrow, the Castle Keep, the room where everything is stored, and everything is absolutely in order. He says:

[T]he soil was very loose and sandy, and had literally to be hammered and pounded into a firm state to serve as a wall for the beautifully vaulted chamber. But for such tasks the only tool I possess is my forehead. So I had to run with my forehead thousands and thousands of times, for whole days and nights, against the ground, and I was glad when the blood came, for that was a proof that the walls were beginning to harden; and in that way, as everybody must admit, I richly paid for my Castle Keep. . . .

It is not so pleasant, however, when as sometimes happens, you suddenly fancy, starting up from your sleep, that the present distribution of your stores is completely and totally wrong, might lead to great dangers, and must be set right at once, no matter how tired or sleepy you may be; then I rush, then I fly, then I have no time for calculation; and although I was about to execute a perfectly new, perfectly exact plan, I now seize whatever my teeth hit upon and drag it or carry it away, sighing, groaning, stumbling, and even the most haphazard change in the present situation, which seems so terribly dangerous, can satisfy me. . . . Besides, it is stupid but true that one's self-conceit suffers if one cannot see all one's stores together, and so, at one glance know how much one possesses [pp. 328–330].

And then he says: "No, if one takes it by and large, I have no right to complain that I am alone, have nobody that I can trust. I certainly lose nothing by that and probably spare myself trouble. I can only trust myself and my burrow" (p. 338).

The troubled beast describes the impossibility of his achieving any sense of safety, endlessly imagining outside beasts that threaten to enter his burrow. Each new security measure leads to new possibilities of hazard in endless sequence, and he experiences increasing frenzy and disorganization as he is unable to quell his conviction of possible unknown attackers who may be intruding on his space. He experiences the gradual collapse of his defenses.

This is a good description of the paranoid character as it appears in many analyses; rather more complete, but entirely consonant with the DSM-III-R description (APA, 1987). (1) At almost every moment one's very life is at stake. (2) One's entire psychic life is devoted to defense against imminent attack and endless anxious vigilance is required. No space or energy is left for pleasure. Peace or certainty lasts only a moment. At the same time fear and passivity are ferociously denied. (3) The surface is all facade and the real life is underground, secret, not available to scrutiny. There is enormous pride in the capacity to disguise intentions, hide meanings, keep secrets. (4) There is great pleasure in feeling that one is smarter than one's enemies. Keenness of mind is valued for its own sake. (5) Murderous oral cannibalistic thoughts, eat or be eaten, are omnipresent. However, every aggressive intention feels as if it is only defensive. (6) Enemies are outside and inside. (7) The edifice of defense and attack is constructed entirely with the efforts of one's mind, the forehead. The achievement is solely one's own; no one else has helped. (8) The life is totally isolated, but malignant others are constantly imagined. (9) No defense feels adequate. Inner reproach cannot be laid to rest, and failure and danger are always imminent. (10) Obsessional defenses bolster paranoid construction, as Melanie Klein pointed out in 1932 (p. 41). Finally, one would conclude that the paranoid life is a hard one.

With this view of paranoia in mind, I would like to do two things, neither of them new. I would like to place paranoid defenses within the context of our growing knowledge of preoedipal object relations, infantile narcissistic needs, and masochistic defenses, and to show how aspects of paranoia are important parts of most analyses, often requiring specific address. From a somewhat different perspective, Meissner (1978, 1986) has advanced this view in considerable detail.

It is part of the history of psychoanalysis that clinical characteristics studied originally for their pathological meanings and consequences were later restudied with an emphasis on their role in normal development and their functioning as an aspect of health. Narcissism has most recently received this revision, due in large part to the work of Kohut (1977), who gave special emphasis to the healthy aspects of narcissism. Brenner (1959) and a succession of later workers on masochism, including myself (Cooper, 1984, 1988, 1989), have established masochistic tendencies also as an aspect of ordinary (i.e., healthy or normal) characterologic functioning. Masochistic tendencies are not only ubiquitous, but masochistic defenses regularly serve important purposes in character formation. Obviously the same can be said for all of the characterologic disorders and traits—histrionic, obsessional, and so on. In these discussions we have sometimes blurred whether we are talking about precisely the same mechanisms in differing degrees or whether we are merely noticing similarities of some of the outer manifestations. When we label somebody histrionic do we mean that they always have both exhibitionistic tendencies toward outward affective display and a tendency toward repression or dissociation, or do we mean only the former? Similarly, when we discuss obsessional tendencies, do we mean only orderliness, stinginess, and stubborn control, or do we also mean the internal struggle over defiance and passivity? I suggest that the dynamic, as well as the phenomenology, is present even in the mild cases. Like any other character trait, paranoid mechanisms are ubiquitous, serve important adaptive functions, as well as being a source of pathological distortions, and at points in the course of analysis they come to the forefront of attention.

There is no need here to review Freud's ideas on paranoia in any detail, but I will mention a few papers by Freud and others to emphasize something that we all know today—that there is within Freud (1911) a view of paranoia quite distinct from that of the Schreber case. In 1932, many years after Freud wrote his analysis of Schreber's book, he wrote his ground-breaking paper on "Female Sexuality," in which, for the first time, he acknowledged the critical role of preoedipal development and conflict in understanding the psyche. Freud said, "Our insight into this early, pre-Oedipus, phase in girls comes to us as a surprise, like the discovery, in another field, of the Minoan-Mycenean civilization behind the civilization of Greece" (p. 226). He went on:

> Nor have I succeeded in seeing my way through any case completely, and I shall therefore confine myself to reporting the most general findings and shall give only a few examples of the new ideas which I have arrived at. Among these is a suspicion that this phase of attachment to the mother is especially intimately related to the aetiology of hysteria, which is not surprising when we reflect that both the phase and the neurosis are characteristically feminine, and further, that in this dependence on the mother we have the germ of later paranoia in women. For this germ appears to be the surprising, yet regular, fear of being killed (?devoured) by the mother. It is plausible to assume that this fear corresponds to a hostility which develops in the child towards her mother in consequence of the manifold restrictions imposed by the latter in the course of training and bodily care and that the mechanism of projection is favoured by the early age of the child's psychical organization [p. 227].

A year later, in his *New Introductory Lectures* (1933) he expanded this insight and writing on "Femininity": "we discover the fear of being murdered or poisoned, which may later form the core of a paranoic illness, already present in this pre-Oedipus period, in relation to the mother" (p. 120). While Freud conservatively confined his considerations to women, today we recognize this conflict as an aspect of every individual's psychic organization. This is also, of course, the nidus of Melanie Klein's constructions, which were being elaborated at the same time (*The Psychoanalysis of Children* was published in 1932). Because her work on paranoid formation is so well known I will assume its presence in this discussion and will briefly mention some parallel contributions.

Sandor Ferenczi, in his *Clinical Diary*, entry of April 10, 1932, made a similar point. Under the heading of "Erotomania as the basis of all paranoia" he tried to understand grandiose delusional formation as a narcissistic defense against the traumatic loss of the love object. He said:

Being loved, being the center of the universe, is the natural emotional state of the baby, therefore it is not a mania but an actual fact. The first disappointments in love (weaning, regulation of the excretory functions, the first punishments through a harsh tone of voice, threats, even spankings) must have, in every case, a traumatic effect, that is, one that produces psychic paralysis from the first moment. The resulting disintegration makes it possible for new psychic formations to emerge. In particular, it may be assumed that a splitting occurs at this stage. The organism has to adapt itself, for example, to the painful realities of weaning, but psychic resistance against it desperately clings to memories of an actual past and lingers for a shorter or longer period in the hallucination: nothing has happened, I am still loved the same as before (hallucinatory omnipotence). All subsequent disappointments, later on in one's love life, may well regress to this wish-fulfillment [p. 83].

In other words, all losses revive the trauma of original narcissistic loss and awaken reparative regressive revivals of the state of narcissistic blissful grandeur, but now in the form of paranoid grandiosity.

Fairbairn, writing in 1941, further diminishing the centrality of the Oedipus complex in psychic development in favor of preoedipal development, proposed (p. 258) that the oedipal situation is primarily sociological rather than psychological, and that all psychopathology results from the hazards of the unconditional dependent identification of the infant with the object, and the life and death choice involved in coping with frustrations by the object (p. 268). He saw paranoia not as a stage of fixation, but as a technique characterized by externalization (excretion) of the internalized object, not just of inner impulses (p. 257). At the end of his paper Fairbairn says: "Even the most 'normal' person must be regarded as having schizoid [i.e. paranoid] potentialities at the deepest levels" (p. 279).

So much for history. I obviously have selected my few authorities to make a point. Viewed in the light of the emphasis on the critical nature of the preoedipal phase in psychic development, and the shift in Freud from a psychology of impulse to a psychology of object relations, we may suggest (and I have done that in an earlier paper; Cooper [1986]) that in paranoia, underlying the original emphasis on the projection of unacceptable homosexual wishes and castration anxiety of the Schreber analysis we find: (1) terror over inner passivity, stressed particularly in "Analysis Terminable and Interminable"

(Freud, 1937, p. 252; Cooper, 1987); (2) terror and fury over the loss of narcissistic intactness occasioned by perceived loss and failure of perfect mothering, and consequent fears of loss of capacity to maintain self-esteem; (3) terror of the building murderous rage that accompanies these fears; (4) the defensive projection of this rage onto the external world, beginning with the mother. Freud, Abraham, Klein, Ferenczi, Fairbairn, Bergler, Bak, Kernberg, Blum, myself, and many others, have seen paranoia as a part of the responses to the inevitable mortifications to the narcissism that sustains infantile self-esteem. If this is the core of paranoia, as this reading of Freud suggests, then of course we will find the mark of these conflicts in every variety of character formation, but especially in the narcissistic-masochistic character, as I have been describing that entity since 1973. What gives a particular conflict or character its paranoid flavor is not the content alone, but, as Franz Kafka and David Shapiro (1965) have described, the extent to which certain specific cognitive styles and uses of projection shape the defenses against the narcissistic hurt and masochistic guilt. Paranoid thinking implies a fixed preconception of the malevolent nature of the world and its objects, or at least of specific objects, and an intolerance for personal responsibility; faults and imperfections are always the result of the malign activities of others.

While we know astonishingly little yet about the specificity of choice of neurosis, Drew Westen (1990), in an important recent paper on empirical research on the theory of borderline object relations, makes several points about our knowledge of development that are germane to an understanding of paranoia. As Emde (1981, 1988) has done before, Westen is suggesting a "new look" to our psychoanalytic understanding of all psychic functioning, one that I endorse. Research suggests the following:

1. We have underrated the role of cognitive style and cognitive deficits in understanding character development generally and specifically the "splitting" or "lack of capacity to tolerate ambivalence" so characteristic of both the borderline and the paranoid. These are best understood as results of the impact of deficits in affect regulation on cognition; specifically, deficits in the control of the impact of high affective arousal on cognitive processing. While these deficits arise at a variety of developmental junctures from infancy throughout adolescence and beyond, nonetheless, "The affective quality of the object world and the capacity to invest in other people are fundamentally

shaped in the pre-oedipal years, so that disruptive or abusive attachments are highly pathogenic'' (Weston, 1990, p. 689). Borderlines and paranoids do not develop the cognitive abilities to counteract dysphoric affects with positive cognitions (e.g., the ability to tell themselves that all is not lost after a bad event). In my view, the paranoid pervasive sense of calamity is also sustained by the grandiose and masochistic conviction that each bit of injustice that befalls one is specifically meted out by a cruel object to torture the innocent individual who would be perfectly, autarchically self-sufficient without this malign interference. This affective, object-relational origin of the paranoid's rigid, blaming, distorted causal cognitive style becomes fixed, secondarily autonomous, and in adult paranoid behavior it represents a deficit, not simply a conflictual compromise, and is not responsive to interpretation alone. Change requires the full weight of prolonged transferential experience with the uniquely persistent and consistent analyst, and the eroding effects of cognitive dissonance within the safety of the analytic setting, as well as the structured and motivational shifts occurring in the course of analysis.

2. Object relations are the result of a number of separate and distinct developmental lines; for example, specific and generalized self and object representations, representations of social interactions, understanding of social causality (that is, what causes people to think, feel, and act as they do), capacity for mature cathexis or emotional investment in the self and others (Weston, 1990). The cognitive, affective, and motivational processes that constitute object relations are at least partly independent, and pathology may exist differently in each mode (Weston, 1990). Paranoids, for example, may have highly distorted object representations, accurate representations of social interactions, and an inaccurate understanding of affective meanings. The patients whom I am discussing here are, at particular times and under particular circumstances, *also* paranoid; it is not their primary character trait.

3. Systematic child observation requires that we abandon our traditional global view of developmental stages, as well as the idea that infantile stages could be reconstructed from adult treatment—a point also strongly made by Emde (1981, 1988). In this view, borderline object relations are not identical to the object relations of toddlers, and adult paranoid syndromes are not identical to infant or child projections. Whether we are viewing narcissistic, masochistic, paranoid, or

borderline pathology, we are not in the presence of an arrest of normal growth—neither simple fixation nor regression—but we are observing pathological growth. No matter how primitive wish-fear-defense-affect-cognition-structural configurations may appear to us, they are never simply infantile.

For example, Rorschach research indicates that borderlines, in contrast to depressives and normals, make their most cognitively advanced attributions of intention on figures regarded as malevolent rather than benign. Malevolence of this degree of complexity of form is not simply a preoedipal issue, but requires development well past latency. I suspect this finding on borderlines would apply equally to the more severe narcissistic patients using paranoid defenses. Unlike borderline patients these patients clearly separate self and other, do not have identity diffusion, and maintain a far greater degree of object constancy, but while the malevolence of the object is fixed, maturation confers greater complexity and conviction to the object relation.

This fine dissection of the complexity and individual variability of the object relational, cognitive, and affective deficits that we encounter clinically helps us to understand the various levels of paranoid functioning, its waxing and waning under different conditions of psychic stress, and the compatibility of primitive affective and cognitive features with high level social functioning. Paranoia as it appears in ordinary analyses is not a constant, but is a quality that appears under specific conditions of conflict for that patient.

I shall try to illustrate some of these points with a clinical vignette.

A highly successful professional man in his late thirties began analysis because he was not getting anywhere in his desire to be married, and didn't know what the trouble was. He had seen another analyst for two months but quit when he concluded the analyst was cold, stupid, and sadistic, and he couldn't stand the withholding and the demand that he speak.

He described his family as close, loving, and completely ordinary, expressing the fear that he might fail in analysis because analysis was supposed to make him hate his mother and he was not sure he had any reason to do that. He was an only child of middle-class parents, the father a successful businessman, the mother a housewife. He was the apple of their eye, and was expected to be perfect. He had no difficulty describing that the mother was expert at suggesting that any misbehavior on his part would lead to her death. When, in his early teens, she developed a carcinoma of the breast and required a mastectomy, he was convinced he was to blame, a conviction he still retained. The father, less overt in his guilt-induction, shared with his son the feeling that the mother was fragile, and great care should be exercised to be sure that she was never upset.

After several preliminary interviews, I recommended analysis, and he thought I might be smarter or livelier than his previous analyst and he was willing to go ahead. He expressed his conviction that because he was so bright, he would figure it out quickly, and he would set a record for speedy analysis. On the other hand, he voiced deep concerns that he would turn out to be hopelessly psychotic and untreatable. Asked about his fear of psychosis, he could not elaborate, other than to say that he must be crazy if he hadn't been able to figure his life out better than he did. He wanted to be a person with a wife and family, so why wasn't he?

He described himself as a worrier as a child. He remembers feeling anxious and telling his parents, perhaps as young as 4 or 5, "I'm worried." And indeed worrying was a major part of his personality, as it was of his mother's. "Worrying," an acceptable adult family trait, was a tolerable substitute for acknowledging that he was frightened. He was exceptionally bright as a child, had friends, but preferred to be alone. He described trying to get his mother to make excuses for him, when the other children called and asked him out to play, but denied any fears of the other children.

He was pleasant, friendly, likeable, had a lively sense of humor, in fact, he went out of his way to be sure that I knew he was witty, was successful in his work, and well liked, and that he had a circle of friends that dated back to childhood, about whom I never learned any details for almost two years of analysis. It emerged over time that no one knew him intimately. At considerable inconvenience he lived in a neighborhood close to where he had grown up, and where his parents still were.

The first sessions on the couch were striking. He lay down, changing his position frequently in almost convulsive jerky movements, issuing barklike sounds as he began to say something and withdrew his beginning communication. He was acutely uncomfortable, with a paralyzing inability to permit himself to make a coherent communication to me. Inquiry as to what this was about revealed consciously that either he had several topics in mind and couldn't decide which was more worthy of my attention, or the things that came to mind were not appropriate topics—too trivial and nothing that I would be interested in—or he was thinking about problems he had left behind at work and that surely was not a topic, or he could not find a way to phrase his communication in a sufficiently literary style. He prided himself on being articulate and he was angry with himself whenever he spoke an ungrammatical sentence, or felt the grammatical construction was ungraceful. It was clear that he was unable to muster the degree of trust and control that would allow him to drop some of his critical faculties. Lest there be doubt about at least one level of his conflict, he came in one session, threw himself on the couch, fell into his barking, squirming routine, and said, "You'd think after I come in bursting to get something out and plop myself down like that I'd come out with something big and juicy rather than the piddling little stuff I have." When I said that sounded as if he were talking of a bowel movement, he gave a great guffaw, enjoying my absurdity, but obviously relaxed and relieved to be understood.

Aware that he had left one analysis because he could not tolerate the anxiety of the analytic setting, I was careful not to let a silence go on very long, and not to leave him with a feeling of losing the power struggle he was creating. As always with paranoia, one finally cannot win. My interventions were seen as my one-upping him, but this was not as anxiety-provoking as the helplessness he felt if a silence continued. It is important to recognize that for patients of this type, the analytic setting seems designed to excite paranoia. The analyst is out of the patient's line of sight behind his defenseless back, not answering questions, and the patient is in the impossible position of being asked to trust the good intentions of someone unknown and invisible. Paranoia in the analytic situation confronts the analyst with a delicate balance. Any abrupt attempt to interpret a defense arouses all the prior convictions of the imminence and inevitability of attack, and defenses are strengthened, since the patient's fantasy of attack has now been substantiated. Secret-keeping is a routine aspect of paranoid behavior, representing both the shame the patient experiences about so many aspects of his inner life, the malevolence he expects from the analyst, and the aggressive attempt to tease the analyst and frustrate him, attempting to goad him into attack, and thereby proving the a priori truth of the analyst's malignancy. Great patience is required in the face of this hostile teasing, since almost any premature activity on the part of the analyst confirms the patient's aggressive projections. He withheld important information about sex, self-image, feelings about his body, feelings toward me. Again, I want to underscore that this outwardly friendly, gregarious man would not have been diagnosed paranoid or borderline by any nosologic system. The analytic situation brought out prominent paranoid defenses that were otherwise well contained.

Over the next several months he relaxed somewhat, his movements on the couch diminished markedly, and he could begin to tolerate silences. At one point he said, "To me it's obvious that if two people are in a room and not talking to each other they are angry at each other. I'm an outsider in your room—I don't share your thoughts and activities. Things that interest me I'm sure don't genuinely interest you. I can't believe that anyone would actually feel as I do and share my interests. I'm self-centered, and I'm lonely." He reviewed how impossible it was for him to conceive of intimacy with another human being; he could only hope to appease them, but they could never enter his world. This man was an unusually able, dedicated, and caring professional, but inwardly his concern for his clients was indistinguishable from his need to control them, and the conviction that if they didn't do well, it was a scheme to make him guilty and anxious. (Later in the analysis he said, "It's a terrible thing for me to realize that I'm not so dedicated to my clients, but only to my not being embarrassed. If I'm on holiday and a colleague of mine screws up with one of my clients I'm relieved and I don't feel bad about the client at all. I'm only worried that I shouldn't be shamed.")

The patient had been a humanities scholar before beginning his professional training, and had a lively interest in drama. This man with a subtle appreciation of literature was entirely unable to tolerate any ambiguity or ambivalence in himself or in his relationships, insisting that they be black or white. Also his belief in magic and superstition was prominent. It was difficult for him to talk about anything bad (e.g., sickness or accidents) because talking about it would make it come true. He literally had to find a piece of wood to knock on if we mentioned a possible misfortune. These clearly obsessional devices covered the more primitive aspects of his paranoid fantasy.

He lived in a crude, split, inner world of good and evil. If he revealed a negative thought to me, it was absolutely certain that I would retaliate ferociously and instantly. He thought that was an evidence of his craziness, but he also believed it to be true. He was convinced that if we ever found out what he was really like, I would give up the analysis, unable to "stomach" him, and he would have to leave because he would turn out to be psychotic. It was a year and a half into the analysis before he could let me know that he had fantasies of my dropping dead in my chair and he would have to administer CPR. He could tell me this only after a colleague of his, also in analysis, told the patient that he had those fantasies and had told his analyst. Having told me, he said, "Don't take it to heart, I don't mean it," and "maybe I should leave now, because you certainly won't be in a very good mood towards me for the rest of the session. Who could stand someone who had those thoughts about him? What do you need that for?" This was a rather precise mirror of his view that he could tolerate no attack upon himself and therefore needed to hold everyone at bay lest they find out who he was.

At the same time that he seemed concerned with pleasing me, he had great difficulty paying my bills. In an almost comic routine, he described writing the check and not being able to find it five minutes later; writing another one and putting it in his shirt pocket, and then sending the shirt to the laundry; writing a check while sitting in the waiting room, but when he finds that my secretary isn't there, he decides not to give it to me despite my suggestion that he pay me directly (too crass), and of course forgets to give it to her later, and so on. He described that he does this in every area of his life, pushing his defiance of rules to the brink, and counting on "magic" to rescue him from consequences. "I'm always innocent. But one day my luck will run out, and you will rise in anger against me, maybe because you're starving because I didn't pay you, and you'll demand payment. I can't imagine that the rules are enough reason to insist on my doing something. So what if the check is late. But if you need it I'll get it for you." I said, "You are above the rules and give crumbs to helpless people. All the power lies with you." "Exactly."

This mixture of paranoid, narcissistic, masochistic, and obsessional features is a common presentation of analytic patients. The extent of paranoid suspicion and rage is often underestimated, commingled as it is with the patient's narcissistic fears of humiliation, and obsessional defenses designed to control and hide the extent of his malignant expectations. Warfare is usually carried on at the level of guerilla resistance rather than nuclear explosions, although occasional cold paranoid fury may burst through.

Later in the analysis after a relatively silent session in which he lay motionless on the couch, he said, "You did what you wanted. You beat me. Satisfied? It won't happen again." Paranoia in these patients represents an available mode that can appear in varying degrees of intensity, whenever there is a threat to higher-level narcissistic defenses. It is not a pathological island in a sea of healthy function. In this patient the relatively polite, ironic, aggressive style which only occasionally broke into overt rage, reflected his mother's masked, martyred, relentlessly aggressive demand that he be an endless source of satisfaction to her—and nothing else.

Oedipal conflicts were apparent on the surface. For example, without my knowledge, he began to use the phone in the resident mailroom near my office to make business calls if he was early. One day there was a notice on the mailroom door that the room was to be kept locked, and he was convinced that I had had that notice put up just to keep him out. He said, "I don't blame you. Next thing I would have had my feet on your desk and you would have thrown me out." When I asked him if he thought I was afraid to tell him directly if I didn't want him using the mailroom phone he said, "Why would you want to create such a frightening situation?" After a moment's pause he said, "You mean maybe I provoke frightening situations," and then said, "You think it's not so frightening."

However, the deeper, less available target of his anger and source of his fear was the female. During the early part of the analysis he complained endlessly about all the women calling him for dates, none of whom he was interested in. He dated someone nearly every weekend, angry, but afraid to say no to them, and believing that somehow I thought it would be good for him. When he realized that I did not require that he make dates and was interested mainly in his feelings of victimization by these women, he stopped dating. Subsequent inquiry about his masturbatory life led to a slightly surprised and offended air—clearly that was none of my business—and no reply. He knew that I meant to shame him and his paranoid defenses hardened.

Telling me a masturbation fantasy was far more difficult than telling me a dream in which a man and woman are going to have a physical fight. She's tough and wiry, the man is ordinary. The woman is the odds-on favorite to win. They go into a closed room and the man emerges, looking bloody and battered, but when they look in the woman is dead. It is clear that she was beaten unfairly—she has been bludgeoned with a lead pipe. Furthermore, there has been some kind of torture—a rope with knots has been passed from her mouth and out of her anus. She is hoisted on the rope and left to die—murdered and mutilated. He says images of mutilation have appeared before. "It makes me a little shaky, says something about me—something nasty." He adds, "I felt nauseated yesterday (before the dream) and was embarrassed by my mother's excessive concern." "I was empathic with the man in my dream who was doing the bludgeoning. I knew he planned to mutilate her. How did I get so crazy?"

While the patient overtly identified with the victorious man in the dream, it became clear that he saw himself as my feminized victim, as well as of any woman who is close to him. Being closed in a room with me required that he be always on guard against my perverse and spiteful "tricks" and power.

The patient then discussed his analysis and his original expectation that there would be a catharsis which would cure him. He now felt he was getting in deeper and deeper and maybe he was really crazy. In fact, he was not at all psychotic, but being crazy, although terrifying, was an acceptable, because blameless, explanation for behaviors that he could not alter, explain, or accept.

While projected rage is always present, projection for the everyday paranoid has less to do with emptying the self of unacceptable contents than it has to do with explaining away to a ferocious superego the reasons for one's sicknesses and failures. Someone to blame is a critical requirement for these patients. One can hear the child's cry, "It's not my fault. It's your fault. You made me do it." The paranoid object for the less severe paranoid is primarily the projection of the desired but unattained powerful destructive self representation, combined with the primitive distorted malignant objects created early in life as rationalization for why one is not able to avoid all frustration. Narcissism is salvaged in the form of blame. "I'd be fine if that monster, wizard, evil genius weren't out to get me. If I were up against an ordinary human being I would win." This is the claim, in one or another form, of every frustrated baby coming to grips with the limits of its autonomy, and the claim of every narcissistic-masochistic character explaining before an accusing inner conscience why he is not meeting

147

the standards of the ego ideal. This blaming defense easily blends into magical thinking. Only secondarily in these patients is the paranoid object either the repository of bad inner contents, or the projection of an unassimilated internal object. The relentless harshness of the superego's shaming accusations is projected onto an external world in which one is innocent victim and masochistic provocateur. All masochism has a paranoid element to it, with the conviction of being the victim of another person or of a malignant fate aimed at oneself. Blaming may be the universal paranoid mechanism.

In the paranoid, in contrast to Borderline Personality Disorder, the paranoid object relation does not rupture. The self and the object are stable, and identity, rather than being diffused, is maintained through the relationship to the powerful object. The self is defined by the enemy, giving it its substance and importance, and providing the hostile object relationship that, no matter how frightening, is still less dangerous than either the intrusion of intimacy, or the horror of inner empty isolation. The full extent of this patient's paranoid isolation, well hidden by his bonhomie and social facade, was not appreciated by me until well into his analysis. He truly lived in his burrow. The developing transference, of course, both provoked the paranoid fear of intrusion and provided the beginning confidence to be able to risk exposure. The need of patients at some points in the analysis to feel that the analyst is malignantly withholding, or torturing, or controlling, represents the attempts to experience oneself as powerful enough to be yielding only to an object of such grand dimensions, to assure oneself that the external world is exactly as predicted, and to protect a fragile self from the hazards of intimacy. It is at these times that the analyst is likely to experience countertransferential boredom, withdrawal, counterattack, inadequacy, and blame.

What I have tried to do in this paper is to demonstrate that paranoid defenses are a very common part of the structure of the narcissistic-masochistic character and of character pathology generally. Paranoid constructions may be a minor or major part of the patient's character, and our treatment strategies will differ accordingly, but it is useful to recognize how common they are, how intimately connected with narcissistic and masochistic pathology, and how enticing paranoid challenges are to countertransferential counterattack.

The full acceptance of paranoid defenses as a significant, although sometimes subtle, aspect of the defensive structure in character pathology will better attune us to the ways in which paranoid processes influence the presentation of the patient's suffering, the transference, and our responsiveness.

REFERENCES

American Psychiatric Association (1987), *Diagnostic and Statistical Manual of Mental Disorders*, 3rd ed. rev. (DSM-III-R). Washington, DC: American Psychiatric Press.

Brenner, C. (1959), The masochistic character: Genesis and treatment. *J. Amer. Psychoanal. Assn.*, 7:197–226.

Cooper, A. M. (1984), The unusually painful analysis: A group of narcissistic-masochistic characters. In: *Psychoanalysis: The Vital Issues*, Vol. 2, ed. J. E. Gedo & G. H. Pollock. New York: International Universities Press, pp. 45–67.

—— (1986), What men fear: The facade of castration anxiety. In: *The Psychology of Men*, ed. G. I. Fogel, F. M. Lane, & R. S. Liebert. New York: Basic Books, pp. 89–106.

—— (1987), Comments on Freud's "Analysis Terminable and Interminable." In: *On Freud's 'Analysis Terminable and Interminable'*, ed. J. Sandler. New Haven: Yale University Press, International Psychoanalytical Association Educational Monographs, No. 1, pp. 127–148.

—— (1988), The narcissistic-masochistic character. In: *Masochism: Current Psychoanalytic Perspectives*, ed. R. A. Glick & D. I. Meyers. Hillside, NJ: Analytic Press, pp. 117–138.

—— (1989), Narcissism and masochism: The narcissistic-masochistic character. *Psychiatric Clin. N.A.*, 12:541–552.

Emde, R. N. (1981). Changing models of infancy and the nature of early development: Remodeling the foundation. *J. Amer. Psychoanal. Assn.*, 29:179–219.

—— (1988), Development terminable and interminable. 1. Innate and motivational factors from infancy. *Internat. J. Psycho-Anal.*, 69:23–42.

Fairbairn, W. R. (1941), A revised psychopathology of the psychoses and psychoneuroses. *Internat. J. Psycho-Anal.*, 22:250–279.

Ferenczi, S. (1933), *The Clinical Diary of Sandor Ferenczi*, ed. J. Dupont, trans. M. Balint & N. Z. Jackson. Cambridge, MA: Harvard University Press, 1988.

Freud, S. (1911), Psycho-analytic notes on an autobiographical account of a case of paranoia (dementia paranoides). *Standard Edition*, 12:3–82. London: Hogarth Press, 1958.

—— (1932), Female sexuality. *Standard Edition*, 21:223–243. London: Hogarth Press, 1961.

—— (1933), New Introductory Lectures on Psycho-Analysis. *Standard Edition*, 22:3–182. London: Hogarth Press, 1964.

—— (1937), Analysis terminable and interminable. *Standard Edition*, 23:211–253. London: Hogarth Press, 1964.

Kafka, F. (1923), The Burrow. In: *The Complete Stories*. New York: Schocken, 1971, pp. 325–359.

Klein, M. (1932), *The Psychoanalysis of Children*. New York: Grove Press, 1960.

—— (1935), A contribution to the psychogenesis of manic-depressive states. *Internat. J. Psycho-Anal.*, 16:145–174.

Kohut, H. (1977), *The Restoration of the Self*. New York: International Universities Press.

Meissner, W. W. (1978), *The Paranoid Process*. New York: Jason Aronson.

—— (1986), *Psychotherapy and the Paranoid Process*. Northvale, NJ: Jason Aronson.

Shapiro, D. (1965), *Neurotic Styles*. New York: Basic Books.

Westen, D. (1990), Towards a revised theory of borderline object relations: Contributions of empirical research. *Internat. J. Psycho-Anal.*, 71:661–694.

10

Do Patients with Paranoid Personality Disorder Seek Psychoanalysis?

John M. Oldham, M.D.
Andrew E. Skodol, M.D.

Paranoia is a word applied in many different contexts, ranging from an attitude in everyday human interactions to a type of severe psychotic illness. It has been described as a universal component of the intrapsychic developmental process, that is, the paranoid position described by Melanie Klein (Segal, 1964), and as a manifestation of regression in individuals, social systems, or groups.

Diagnostically, paranoia is a common component of character pathology, varying from the predominant feature of the pathology to an occasional type of interpersonal reaction. Psychoanalysts have endorsed a much broader view of the paranoid process than Freud's psychosexual formulation described in the Schreber case (Freud, 1911). Freud himself, in other writings (Freud, 1896), referred to the role of hostility in some forms of paranoia, and Abraham (1924), still utilizing a psychosexual framework, saw paranoia as a regressive reactivation of anal sadism. The object relations theorists, following the work of Klein, emphasized the projective process in paranoia as a protection against the internalized bad object. The concept of paranoia as a defense has been extended more recently by Kernberg (1975) and others, in formulations of borderline personality organization, to encompass the concept of projective identification as a mechanism to deal with intense aggression.

Psychodynamic formulations such as these are applied to patients with varying degrees of paranoia and with varying diagnoses. According to DSM-III-R (APA, 1987), there are three diagnostic categories centrally characterized by paranoid mechanisms: schizophrenia, paranoid type; delusional (paranoid) disorder; and paranoid personality disorder. Of these, only paranoid personality disorder is generally viewed as a disorder potentially treatable by psychoanalytic methods, and even then only in some cases. More often, paranoia is described in the course of psychoanalytic work as a component of mixed character pathology or as a regressive process emerging in the course of the psychoanalytic process.

Many psychoanalysts have been critical of the phenomenologic approach taken by DSM-III (1980) and DSM-III-R. However, Frances and Cooper argued in 1981 that "psychodynamic psychiatrists need not be particularly alarmed or troubled by the descriptive approach of DSM-III," adding that "to facilitate communication the profession must also learn to play by DSM-III rules." They went on to say, "if classifications are arbitrary, and to a degree, all of them must be, it is a major advance to have everyone following the same conventions and speaking the same language" (p. 1202). However, the usefulness of applying a DSM-III diagnostic framework to analytic work has been questioned by many psychoanalysts. In a panel report entitled "Psychoanalytic Contributions to Psychiatric Nosology" (Panel, 1987), several views were expressed including that of Michels, who was quoted as saying "we need a truce between descriptive and dynamic psychiatrists. We have much to learn, each from the other, and little to gain from fighting over symbols" (p. 697). And, in the same year, Simons (1987) reviewed the strengths and weaknesses of DSM-III from a psychoanalytic perspective, concluding that:

> DSM-III holds out the promise of truly advancing and stimulating our clinical work by asking us to first observe what the various struggles are that seem to be occurring in the lives of our patients, as reflected in specific symptoms and behaviors (the descriptive model), before prematurely leaping to various theories that attempt to explain how

those symptoms occur (the dynamic model) or why they came to be (the developmental model) [p. 585].

It is our belief that psychoanalytic assessment, process, and outcome research can be done more effectively if psychoanalytic researchers get into diagnostic step with the psychiatric research community at large. However flawed DSM-III may be, there is inevitably less heterogeneity in most patient groups defined by its diagnostic criteria than by nonstandardized clinical judgment alone. The advantage of having psychoanalytic patients assessed by DSM-III-based methods is that research to compare psychoanalysis with other forms of treatment can be better designed since, at least, it will be more likely that patient groups being compared are diagnostically similar.

In a series of reports by Weber, Bachrach, and Solomon (1985a,b), Weber, Solomon, and Bachrach (1985), and Bachrach, Weber, and Solomon (1985), attempts were made to characterize psychoanalytic clinic patients and to identify factors associated with the outcome of psychoanalysis. These studies did not, however, utilize DSM-III terminology, and no systematic evaluation procedure was used to establish the presence or absence of diagnoses such as, for example, major depression or paranoid personality disorder, which, among others, could have critical importance in determining both the choice of treatment and its outcome. Many reports exist in the psychoanalytic literature concerning the assessment of analyzability of patients. Here too, however, there is a high degree of inference and subjectivity about the patients being described, without application of standardized assessments based on research diagnostic criteria. Erle and Goldberg in 1984, for example, reported a retrospective study of assessment of analyzability. No standard diagnostic terminology was utilized by these analysts nor was any attempt made retrospectively to apply research diagnostic criteria to the subjects being studied.

Based on a view that a more systematic approach, incorporating standardized assessment methods for the personality disorders based on DSM-III-R criteria, might better inform us about our decisions regarding analyzability and about our predictions as to the course and outcome of analysis, a group of us embarked on a research project at the Columbia Psychoanalytic Center, funded in part by the Fund for Psychoanalytic Research of the American Psychoanalytic Association. The goal of the project involved assessment of 100 patients applying for psychoanalysis at the Center. The patients received the usual evaluation by the admissions service. An admitting psychoanalyst interviewed each patient, completed a clinical narrative, arrived at a clinical diagnosis, and recommended psychoanalysis or some other form of treatment. Independent interviewers, consisting of research psychiatrists, administered semistructured DSM-III-R-based interviews to the patients applying to the Center. The researchers were blind to the clinical evaluation by the admissions service, and the admissions service, in turn, was blind to the research assessment. Instruments used included the Personality Disorder Examination (PDE) (Loranger, Susman, Oldham, and Russakoff, 1985) and the Structured Clinical Interview for DSM-III-R (SCID-I and SCID-II) (Spitzer, Williams, and Gibbon, 1987), for assessing Axis I and Axis II disorders.

In this chapter, we examine and compare applicants for psychoanalysis with paranoid personality disorder with those having other types of personality disorders, and we compare research-based assessments of patients with paranoid PD with standard clinical assessments of the same patients by the admissions service.

TABLE 10.1
Prevalence of Personality Disorders by Personality Disorder Examination (PDE) or Structured Clinical Interview for DSM-III-R (SCID-II) (N = 100).

Personality Disorder	PDE	SCID-II	Either
Paranoid	4	11	12
Schizoid	1	0	1
Schizotypal	0	1	1
Antisocial	4	2	4
Borderline	18	11	24
Histrionic	5	7	10
Narcissistic	6	5	10
Avoidant	16	20	27
Dependent	6	11	14
Obsessive Compulsive	10	16	20
Passive Aggressive	2	5	6
Self-Defeating	14	15	21
Total	86	104	150

Table 10.1 shows the distribution of personality disorders in the 100 patients by the two different methods. As can be seen, 11 patients of the 100 were diagnosed paranoid by SCID-II and only four by PDE.

Three of these patients were diagnosed by both methods so that a total of 12 patients were diagnosed paranoid by either method. We consider the 3 who were positive by both methods as "definite" and the 9 who were positive by only one of the two methods as "probable" for paranoid personality disorder. Many of these patients had coexisting other probable or definite personality disorders as well, along with diagnoses on Axis I.

TABLE 10.2
Demographic Characteristics of Subjects (N = 100).

Characteristic	Subgroup	Number of Psychoanalytic Applicants
Sex	Male	59
	Female	41
Age	16–20 years	0
	21–25	19
	26–30	40
	31–35	18
	36–40	11
	41–45	4
	45 and over	8
Ethnicity	White	88
	African-American	6
	Hispanic	5
	Asian-American	1
Education	Less than high school	0
	High school graduate	0
	Some college	12
	College graduate	88
Marital status	Married	11
	Separated/Divorced	8
	Widowed	0
	Never married	81
Employment	Current	86
	Past year	95

Table 10.2 shows demographic data on the total patient group. The patients are fairly evenly divided between males and females, though more are male. Most of them have never been married, and

are white, currently employed, and college graduates. As shown on Table 10.3, the twelve patients who had paranoid personality disorder by either method are demographically similar to the total sample.

TABLE 10.3
Columbia Psychoanalytic Center Patient Applicants with Paranoid Personality Disorder (N = 12).

	N	%
Male	8	67
Female	4	33
Never Married	10	83
Married	1	8
Separated	1	8
White	11	92
Hispanic	1	8
Currently Employed	12	100
College Graduate or More	11	92
Not College Graduate	1	8

The average number of personality disorders per patient is shown on Table 10.4. Patients with paranoid personality disorder had on the

TABLE 10.4
Average Number of Personality Disorders Per Patient.

	Average Number	
	SCID-II	PDE
Patients with Paranoid PD (N = 12)	2.8	1.8
Patients with other than Paranoid PD (N = 45)	1.2	1.1

average a total of 2.8 personality disorders by SCID-II and 1.8 by PDE, whereas patients with personality disorders other than paranoid had an average of 1.2 coexisting disorders by SCID-II and 1.1 by PDE. Thus, patients with paranoid personality disorder had more severe character pathology, as represented by the number of personality disorder diagnoses made, than patients with other personality disorders.

The distribution of probable or definite Axis II diagnoses in patients with Paranoid PD is shown on Table 10.5. As can be seen, in all cases but two, when patients had other personality disorders in

TABLE 10.5

All Axis II Diagnoses in Patients with Paranoid Personality Disorder by Either PDE or SCID-II.

Case Number:	1	2	3	4	5	6	7	8	9	10	11	12
Paranoid	+	+	+	+	+	+	+	+	+	+	+	+
Schizoid												
Schizotypal										+		
Antisocial												
Borderline		+	+	+	+		+	+	+			+
Histrionic		+					+					
Narcissistic		+		+			+			+	+	
Avoidant									+	+	+	+
Dependent										+	+	+
Obsessive Compulsive								+		+	+	+
Passive Aggressive		+		+			+					

addition to paranoid, they had borderline personality disorder, plus in most cases other disorders in the "Dramatic/Impulsive" cluster (antisocial, borderline, histrionic, or narcissistic) or in the "Anxious/Fearful" cluster (avoidant, dependent, obsessive compulsive, or passive aggressive) of disorders.

TABLE 10.6

SCID-I Diagnoses in Entire Patient Sample (N = 100).

	Current	Lifetime
	N = %	N = %
Mood Disorder	30	73
Psychotic Disorder	0	2
Anxiety Disorder	31	39
Eating Disorder	1	8
Alcohol or Substance Use Disorder	11	47
No Axis I Diagnosis	41	8

Axis I diagnoses in the total patient population are shown on Table 10.6, indicating that 73 percent of the psychoanalytic clinic applicants had a diagnosable mood disorder at some time in their lives, 30 percent of which were currently present at the time of their evaluation at the Center. Thirty-one percent had current anxiety disorders, and 11 percent had current alcohol or other substance use disorders. As shown on Table 10.7, for patients diagnosed paranoid by either method, 42 percent had current mood disorders; this is compared to 28 percent without paranoid PD. Current anxiety and substance

TABLE 10.7

SCID-I Diagnoses in Patients with Paranoid Personality Disorder (N = 12).

	Current		Lifetime	
	N	%	N	%
Mood Disorder	5	42	10	83
Psychotic Disorder	0	0	0	0
Anxiety Disorder	4	33	4	33
Eating Disorder	0	0	2	17
Alcohol or Substance Use Disorder	1	8	7	58

use disorders occurred in 33 and 8 percent, respectively, in paranoid patients, compared to 31 percent and 11 percent of the patients without paranoid PD. None of these Axis I differences is significant.

Table 10.8 compares the Axis I and Axis II diagnoses made by the clinicians and by the research team. Two different psychoanalysts on the admissions service independently evaluated the patient (usually a psychoanalytic candidate in training and a supervising psychoanalyst); both sets of clinical diagnoses on both axes are shown. For contrast, the research diagnoses are shown for the same patients. Axis I diagnoses are by SCID-I and Axis II diagnoses are by either SCID-II or PDE.

It is striking that for all twelve patients who were positive for paranoid personality disorder by either the PDE or the SCID-II, the word *paranoid* does not ever once appear in the routine clinical evaluations recorded by the admissions service. In some cases, when by structured interview paranoid PD was only one of several personality disorders, including borderline PD, it may not have been a particularly prominent component of the psychopathology. Clinicians' diagnoses of borderline personality organization, which encompasses paranoid PD and several other categories in DSM-III-R, may explain their omission of specific reference to paranoid personality. Often, the term *mixed personality disorder* was intended to encompass a range of character pathology, but listings of descriptive features accompanying the "mixed" category never included reference to paranoid features. Often narcissistic or masochistic features were referred to, which could of course contain ingredients of paranoia. Despite differences in diagnostic concepts and terminology, however, one might expect some reference to suspiciousness, mistrustfulness, self-referential thinking, or similar traits or behaviors by the analyst evaluators in these cases; such a reference occurred only once, where "mistrust" was mentioned. Even in the two cases where there were no Axis II diagnoses by structured interviews other than paranoid PD, no mention of paranoia, suspiciousness, or mistrustfulness was recorded by the clinical evaluators.

In the PDE, the threshold for a positive diagnosis of paranoid PD is considerably higher than that of the SCID-II, but in both interviews the questions are fairly specific for paranoid attitudes and thinking. Sample questions from the PDE, for example, include the following:

> Do you keep things to yourself rather than tell others what is on your mind? Is that because you're afraid people may use the information against you?
> Do you refuse to forgive those who have insulted or slighted you?
> Do you often find hidden threats or insults in what others say?
> Have you felt that some people are out to ruin your reputation or bring about your downfall?

And similarly, questions from the SCID-II section on paranoid PD include the following:

> Do you often have to keep an eye out to stop people from using you or hurting you?
> Do you often pick up hidden meanings in what people say or do?
> Do you often get angry because someone has slighted you or insulted you in some way?

These sample questions indicate that, although more so for the PDE than the SCID-II, a positive diagnosis by either method would suggest a significant clinical concern in the area of interpersonal trust.

Finally, we examined which of the clinic applicants were accepted for psychoanalysis and how many of those accepted remained in or completed psychoanalysis. As shown on Table 10.9, only 58 percent of the patients were accepted. Of those, 45 percent are still in or have completed analysis (up to 6 years later); 22 percent chose not to enter

TABLE 10.8
Clinical vs. Research Diagnoses

Case #	Axis	Clinical Diagnoses by Two Different Psychoanalysts	Research Diagnoses	Accepted for Analysis?
1	I	1. Cyclothymia 2. —	Major depression (subthreshold) (ST)	Yes
	II	1. Personality Disorder, Unspecified 2. Dependent Personality	Paranoid PD	
2	I	1. — 2. —	Generalized anxiety disorder (ST); hx of major depression and cannabis dependence	Yes
	II	1. Mixed PD 2. Mixed PD w/narcissistic features	Paranoid, borderline, histrionic, narcissistic, and passive aggressive PDs	
3	I	1. — 2. —	Major depression and dysthymia; hx of alcohol abuse	Yes
	II	1. Obsessive Compulsive Personality with Masochistic Features 2. Mixed Character Disorder w/Obsessional & Masochistic Features	Paranoid and borderline PDs	
4	I	1. — 2. —	Major depression	No
	II	1. Borderline PD 2. Schizoid Personality w/ Borderline Features	Paranoid, borderline, narcissistic, obsessive compulsive & passive aggressive PDs	
5	I	1. Sexual Masochism 2. Impotence, Ego-Dystonic Homosexuality, Possible Fetishism	Bipolar dis. NOS (hypomanic) and obsessive compulsive disorder; hx of alcohol dependence	Yes
	II	1. Mixed PD 2. Neurotic Character w/Masochistic and Narcissistic Features	Paranoid and borderline PDs	

6	I	1. Dysthymia 2. R/O Major Depressive Episodes; Marijuana, Cocaine, and Alcohol Abuse	Adjustment disorder w/depressed mood, cannabis and alcohol dependence (ST); hx of alcohol dependence, stimulant and cocaine abuse	No
	II	1. Borderline Personality 2. —	Paranoid PD	
7	I	1. Prominent Affective Component 2. —	Hx of major depression and cannabis dependence	No
	II	1. Mixed PD w/Narcissistic and Histrionic Features 2. Narcissistic and Depressive Personality Features linked w/some High-level Borderline Pathology	Paranoid, borderline, histrionic, narcissistic, and passive aggressive PDs	
8	I	1. Alcoholism 2. Hx of Depression	Social phobia, obsessive compulsive disorder, alcohol dependence (ST); hx of major depression, panic disorder, anorexia, and bulimia (ST)	No
	II	1. Narcissistic Personality w/ Sadomasochistic and Borderline Features 2. Borderline PD	Paranoid, borderline, avoidant, and obsessive compulsive PDs	
9	I	1. Depression 2. —	Major depression and trichotillomania	No
	II	1. Personality Disorder w/Marked Narcissistic and Masochistic Features 2. Mixed PD w/Narcissistic, Masochistic, and Depressive Features	Paranoid, borderline, and dependent PDs	

161

TABLE 10.8 (continued)

Case #	Axis	Clinical Diagnoses by Two Different Psychoanalysts	Research Diagnoses	Accepted for Analysis?
10	I	1. Major Depression, Recurrent, in Remission 2. Sexual Disorder NOS	Posttraumatic stress disorder; hx of major depression, dysthymia (secondary), and alcohol abuse	No
	II	1. Mixed PD w/Avoidance Features 2. Avoidant Personality Type, r/o Borderline Personality	Paranoid, antisocial, narcissistic, avoidant, and obsessive compulsive PDs	
11	I	1. Anxious, Hx of Depression 2. —	Social phobia; hx of major depression (ST) and obsessive compulsive disorder (ST)	No
	II	1. Obsessive Compulsive 2. Obsessional Personality	Paranoid, narcissistic, avoidant, dependent, and obsessive compulsive PDs	
12	I	1. Cyclothymic Dis.; r/o Bipolar Affective Disorder 2. Cyclothymic Dis.; r/o Major Affective Dis., Mixed Type: Bulimia	Other bipolar disorder, simple phobia, obsessive compulsive disorder and bulimia (ST); hx of alcohol dependence, agoraphobia w/o panic disorder, and anorexia	No
	II	1. Probable Mixed Character Dis. 2. Mixed Character Disorder w/ Masochistic and Passive Dependent Features	Paranoid, borderline, avoidant, dependent, and obsessive compulsive PDs	

TABLE 10.9
Patients Accepted for Analysis (N = 58).

	N	%
Still in or completed analysis	26	45
Began, but dropped out or referred out	17	29
Did not enter analysis	13	22
Other	2	3

analysis; and 29 percent began but dropped out. In contrast, only four of the twelve paranoid patients were accepted for analysis (33%).

Thus, there is a trend that patients with paranoid PD are less likely to be accepted for psychoanalysis than patients not diagnosed paranoid. Furthermore, of the four paranoid patients accepted for analysis, three had only one or two personality disorders. This suggests that patients with paranoid PD who are accepted for analysis have less severe character pathology than those patients with paranoid PD who are not accepted.

Treatment planning did not include the recommendation for analysis in eight of the twelve paranoid cases. Two of these had current major depression by research assessment; one had current bipolar disorder, simple phobia, and obsessive compulsive disorder; one had current social phobia; two had current alcoholism or substance abuse; one had posttraumatic stress disorder; and one had no current Axis I disorder. Of the four accepted, two had current major depression, and the other two had current anxiety disorders, one of whom also had current bipolar disorder. It is difficult, therefore, to discriminate in this small sample between those accepted and those not accepted for analysis based on current Axis I pathology, but Axis I pathology that may well have needed treatment was identified in the clinical diagnoses by the admissions service in only one of the four accepted cases.

In the clinical literature, it is generally accepted that if psychoanalysis is appropriate for a patient with DSM-III-R diagnosable paranoia, the diagnosis will be paranoid personality disorder, and even with these patients, analysis will be appropriate only some of the time. Is that clinical recommendation borne out by the more extensive data collected in this study? Since none of our patients had the Axis I diagnosis of either delusional (paranoid) disorder or schizophrenia, paranoid type, there is no information about what treatment recommendation might have been made in such cases.

Do patients with paranoid personality disorder seek psychoanalysis? According to these data, we would conclude that a sizable minority of patients seeking psychoanalysis may have paranoid personality disorder. In fact, although many more applicants received research diagnoses of avoidant, borderline, and obsessive compulsive personality disorders (Oldham and Skodol, unpublished data), paranoid personality disorder was diagnosed more frequently than any DSM-III-R personality disorder other than Cluster C disorders, except for borderline PD. When patients with paranoid PD seek analysis, are they deemed suitable? Our data suggest that sometimes they are, but only infrequently. Are they then analyzable? The number of patients with paranoid PD is not sufficiently large to answer this question, except to provide four case examples; the diagnostic description of these cases is shown on Table 10.8 (Cases 1, 2, 3, and 5). Case 1 began in analysis in 1987 and reached a successful conclusion in 1992. Case 2 began in 1988 and continues in analysis at the present time (1993). Case 3 began in 1989, but the patient became increasingly depressed in analysis, began to miss sessions, and was ultimately referred for psychotherapy in 1991. Analysis began for case 5 in 1988, but the patient dropped out after only three sessions and was noted to be unmotivated for psychoanalysis.

In conclusion, it appears that a surprising number of patients with paranoid personality disorder seek psychoanalysis. Compared to other applicants for psychoanalysis, patients with paranoid personality disorder often have other personality disorders, especially borderline personality disorder, as well. Compared to applicants with other nonparanoid personality disorders, patients with paranoid PD appear to have more severe character pathology. Despite apparently being unaware of their patients' paranoid traits, clinical evaluators select a few, generally less severe cases for psychoanalysis. And, although our experience is based on only a handful of cases, paranoia in the form of paranoid personality disorder does not seem to be a contraindication for psychoanalysis. Further systematic studies of patients with paranoid personality disorder are needed to more fully understand the role of paranoia in the process of selection for psychoanalysis and the impact of paranoia on the conduct of psychoanalytic treatment and its outcome.

REFERENCES

Abraham, K. (1924), A short study of the development of the libido, viewed in the light of mental disorders. In: *On Character and Libido Development*. New York: Basic Books, 1966.

American Psychiatric Association (1980), *Diagnostic and Statistical Manual of Mental Disorders*, 3rd ed. (DSM-III). Washington, DC: American Psychiatric Press.

―――― (1987), *Diagnostic and Statistical Manual of Mental Disorders*, 3rd ed. rev. (DSM-III-R). Washington, DC: American Psychiatric Press.

Bachrach, H. M., Weber, J. J., & Solomon, M. (1985), Factors associated with the outcome of psychoanalysis (Clinical and methodological considerations): Report of the Columbia Psychoanalytic Center research project, IV. *Internat. Rev. Psychoanal.*, 12:379–389.

Erle, J. B., & Goldberg, D. A. (1984), Observations on assessment of analyzability by experienced analysts. *J. Amer. Psychoanal. Assn.*, 32:715–737.

Frances, A., & Cooper, A. M. (1981), Descriptive and dynamic psychiatry: A perspective on DSM-III. *Amer. J. Psychiatry*, 138:1198–1202.

Freud, S. (1896), Further remarks on the neuro-psychoses of defence. *Standard Edition*, 3:159–185. London: Hogarth Press, 1962.

―――― (1911), Psychoanalytic notes on an autobiographical account of a case of paranoia (dementia paranoides). *Standard Edition*, 12:3–79. London: Hogarth Press, 1958.

Kernberg, O. (1975), *Borderline Conditions and Pathological Narcissism*. New York: Jason Aronson.

Loranger, A. W., Susman, V. L., Oldham, J. M., & Russakoff, L. M. (1985), *Personality Disorder Examination (PDE): A Structured Interview for DSM-III-R Personality Disorders*. White Plains, NY: New York Hospital-Cornell Medical Center, Westchester Division.

Panel (1987), Psychoanalytic contributions to psychiatric nosology. M. L. Peltz (reporter). *J. Amer. Psychoanal. Assn.*, 35:693–711.

Segal, H. (1964), *Introduction to the Work of Melanie Klein*. New York: Basic Books.

Simons, R. C. (1987), Psychoanalytic contributions to psychiatric no-
     sology: Forms of masochistic behavior. *J. Amer. Psychoanal.
     Assn.*, 35:583–608.
Spitzer, R. L., Williams, J. B. W., & Gibbon, M. (1987), *Structured
     Clinical Interview for DSM-III-R*. New York: Biometrics Re-
     search, New York State Psychiatric Institute.
Weber, J. J., Solomon, M., & Bachrach, H. M. (1985), Characteris-
     tics of psychoanalytic clinic patients: Report of the Columbia
     Psychoanalytic Center research project, I. *Internat. Rev. Psy-
     choanal.*, 12:13–24.
————— Bachrach, H. M., & Solomon, M. (1985a), Factors associated
     with the outcome of psychoanalysis: Report of the Columbia
     Psychoanalytic Center research project, II. *Internat. Rev. Psy-
     choanal.*, 12:127–141.
————— ————— ————— (1985b), Factors associated with the outcome
     of psychoanalysis: Report of the Columbia Psychoanalytic Center
     research project, III. *Internat. Rev. Psychoanal.*, 12:251–262.

Name Index

Subject Index

SUBJECT INDEX